CRITICAL DIRECTIONS

A series of criticism selected and edited by
J.R. (Tim) Struthers
Department of English, University of Guelph

The volumes chosen for this series explore directions through which criticism can uphold its most urgent responsibilities: to the honouring of literature and language, to the cultivation of a more profound, more valuable experience of art and life, and to the building of a more enlightened society.

VOLLEYS

CRITICAL DIRECTIONS

*Sam Solecki, John Metcalf
and W.J. Keith*

The Porcupine's Quill

CANADIAN CATALOGUING IN PUBLICATION DATA

Solecki, Sam, 1946-
  Volleys

(Critical directions)
ISBN 0-88984-113-6

1. Canadian literature – History and criticism.
2. Criticism. I. Metcalf, John, 1938- .
II. Keith, W.J. (William John), 1934- .
III. Title. IV. Series.

PS8061.S64 1990   810.9   C90-095754-9
PR9184.6.S64 1990

Published by The Porcupine's Quill, Inc., 68 Main Street, Erin, Ontario NOB 1TO with financial assistance from the Canada Council and the Ontario Arts Council.

Distributed by The University of Toronto Press, 5201 Dufferin Street, Downsview, Ontario M3H 5T8.

Edited for the press by J.R. (Tim) Struthers.

Cover is after a painting, 'Are You Sure You Don't See What You Hear?', acrylic and oil stick on canvas, 1988, by Tony Calzetta.

Printed and bound by The Porcupine's Quill.
The stock is Zephyr laid, and the type, Ehrhardt.

Contents

Acknowledgements

An earlier version of Sam Solecki's essay was published under the title 'Some Kicks Against the Prick: John Metcalf in His Essays' in *The Bumper Book,* ed. John Metcalf (Toronto: ECW, 1986). That material is used here with the permission of ECW Press.

John Metcalf's essay 'Dear Sam' was presented as the conclusion to the 'Coming of Age: John Metcalf and the Canadian Short Story' conference hosted by J.R. (Tim) Struthers at the University of Guelph from November 9 to 12, 1988. This essay is printed here for the first time.

W.J. Keith's essay was written for this volume and is printed here for the first time.

The editor of this volume, J.R. (Tim) Struthers, wishes to thank Laurie Williams for her research assistance, as well as various members of the staff in the Department of English, University of Guelph, for their secretarial assistance.

Some Kicks Against the Prick

Nothing was alien to him, everything repelled him.
  Peter Handke, *A Moment of True Feeling*[1]

WHEN I PUBLISHED John Metcalf's essay 'Without an "E"' in the *Canadian Forum* it generated two kinds of responses. Among the first were the reactions of those readers who took it for granted that Metcalf, if not quite out of his mind, nevertheless represented a viewpoint sufficiently eccentric that he could be ignored. His acerbic comments on Canadian culture, Canadian universities, and Canadian critics were treated as, at best, the ravings of a disgruntled expatriate – he was really English, wasn't he? – longing for the imperial centre because he couldn't get *The Spectator* in Fredericton. Among the second were those who took the slightly more generous view that Metcalf was probably sane but that his one-man attack on some of the more questionable branches of the tree of Canadian culture was vaguely anti-Canadian or, if not that, then in bad taste and certainly badly timed because, after all, 'real' Canadian literature had only recently come into existence, deserved our support, and so on. Some even reminded me that Metcalf was a recent immigrant and that his attacks therefore smacked both of self-interest and, since he had accepted grants and positions as writer-in-residence, ingratitude. Typically Canadian was the reluctance of any of my correspondents to let me put their comments on the magazine's 'Letters' page. I mention this obscure episode from the literary history of one of our monthly journals because I want to discuss Metcalf's essays[2] in the general context of these remarks. For the sake of convenience, I shall group my comments under two headings – 'Curmudgeon and Satirist' (or 'Metcalf as Richler') and 'Style and Self-interest' (or 'Metcalf as Flaubert'). Their significance, I hope, will become clear.

1. Metcalf as Richler

No more bullshit.
Norman Mailer, when running for mayor of New York.

UNTIL THE PUBLICATION of Metcalf's *Kicking Against the Pricks* in 1982, Canadian literature had lacked three essential things: a great critic with a reputation based on his work in Canadian literature, a great writer, and a resident curmudgeon. We're still looking for the first two but the last, I want to suggest, has been filled by Metcalf. At times both Louis Dudek and Mordecai Richler seemed interested but the timing was wrong for each. Canadian literature, then almost non-existent, didn't need a great nay-sayer in the 1950s and early 60s. In the 1980s, by contrast, it has been praying for one. But Dudek also failed because he simply wasn't funny – humour is hardly his calling card – while Richler, although a brilliant social satirist, seemed to realize very early on that for him to satirize Canadian culture and society in the 50s and 60s would be like sending the proverbial destroyer to sink a row-boat. Metcalf, on the other hand, seems to relish the job, bringing to it a sadomasochistic zeal that even Richler would envy. All that's missing is the weekly or bi-weekly column by the last angry almost-young man on some op-ed page or in some weekly magazine.

The essential characteristic of the curmudgeon is opposition. He stands opposed to most of the prevailing political and cultural fashions, trends, and ideas of his society. Above his desk could hang Evelyn Waugh's comment that 'An artist *must* be a reactionary. He has to stand out against the tenor of the age and not go flopping along; he must offer some little opposition.'[3] Usually this means that the curmudgeon as essayist or columnist is a conservative, although unlike the late Philip Larkin he may not be willing to declare that he adores Mrs. Thatcher. But even to mention the latter in this context is misleading because the sort of conservatism or 'reaction' I'm concerned with is not so much political as temperamental; its responses and judgements have their roots less in ideology than in sensibility. The writer I'm thinking of is usually less clear in describing and defining the things of which he approves than those which he dislikes. Approbation is usually extended only to those things associated with an idealized past which often coincides with the author's childhood or with his parents' and grandparents' generations. Disapproval is usually meted out to everything modern from plastic to feminism to mass education to television; the catalogue is almost endless. In Metcalf's case it includes, in addition to the items mentioned, McDonald's, the Group of Seven, small presses, courses in Creative Writing, the federal cabinet, amateur reviewers, the sixties. He summarizes his situation as follows: 'I look upon the world I inhabit with considerable distaste and gloom; I'm beginning to suspect that I may end my days in a loony bin after an unprovoked and murderous assault on a McDonald's hostess' (KAP 204); 'I'm violently in conflict with the dominant nature of North American society and this affords me at varying times great distress and great amusement' (KAP 3). The distress arises in part from the recognition of what has been lost (this is the usual source of conservative gloom from Burke to Leavis since the conservative is haunted by loss in much the same way that the leftist is tormented by possibility); the amusement comes from the sheer absurdity of some aspects of modern life. Metcalf offers an example from literature:

> Everything seems to be splintering. Regional presses – a *disastrous* development. *Great Stories from Saskatoon.* Special interest presses. *Gay Maritime Stories.* Feminist presses.
> Which reminds me. I was looking at a thing called *Fireweed – A Feminist Quarterly.* In the Notes on Contributors at the back it said of one lady, 'she is currently editing an anthology of first-person poems by people who were molested as children'. (KAP 14-15)

This passage also points to some other characteristics of the literary curmudgeon: the writing must be witty and satirical if it is to be anything more than just the grumblings of frustrated reaction; the satire, to be effective, must have both general and particular targets; the curmudgeon as commentator or satirist normally risks controversy. In Metcalf's case one senses that he courts it, realizing that only in a full assault on the petrified establishment can he hope for even a minimum success. He mocks, exaggerates wildly – 'it is debatable whether at least one member of the present cabinet is functionally literate' ('Curate's Egg' 37) – and generalizes in order to provoke but also to establish a potential debate between an entrenched and, for the moment, unquestioned set of opinions and his minority view. Failure in this instance lies not in being attacked in return or even in being actively rejected but in being ignored. The worst thing that the academy's 'sons of dullness' (KAP 151) can do to you is to pretend that they haven't heard you or that you're not worth listening to.

The naming of individuals in Metcalf's essays, then, is part of a strategy to draw 'them' out of the tenured complacency of safe offices onto the neutral white of newspapers and journals: neutral ground with words, the tools of Metcalf's craft, as the only weapons. Let me illustrate Metcalf's provocations with a passage from 'The Curate's Egg':

> The previous edition [of *The Oxford Companion to Canadian Literature*] actually contained an entry on a writer called John Metcalfe; this followed the entry on John Metcalf. The new edition has deleted that mythical Metcalfe but now refers to me as Metacalf.
>
> Can this be *the* Oxford University Press?
>
> Well, no.
>
> On closer examination, it turns out to be Oxford (Canada).
>
> The desire for a Canadian literature overmasters rationality and decency. There are no intellectual depths to which those who boost Canlit indiscriminately will not sink;

some are even busying themselves writing revisionist literary history. Wayne Grady in his preface to *The Penguin Book
of Canadian Short Stories* goes so far as to assert a native
Canadian tradition in story-writing which he claims, quoting David Arnason, as 'the development of the Letter to the
Editor as a specialized literary form'; he attempts, vaguely,
to link to this alleged tradition such contemporary writers
as Alice Munro, Hugh Hood, Mordecai Richler, and Margaret Laurence.

Desperate stuff.

I await, calmly, such future revisionist papers as: 'The
Influence on Richler's Narrative Technique of the Oral
Tradition of the James Bay Cree'.

But there is worse.

Professor Robin Mathews, the Ayatollah Khomeini of
Canlit and a tenured inmate of Carleton University, has, in
one of his amazing books, attacked Morley Callaghan as a
traitor to Canadian-ness *for having succumbed to literary
influence from the* U.S.A. *and for having expressed admiration for
the Great Satan Hemingway.*

The purity of such cultural nationalists scares me. Can
rigorous vegetarianism and persecution be far behind?

It is important that you understand that these are not figures from Canadian writing's lunatic fringe; they are at
Canlit's core. ('Curate's Egg' 38-39)

It's tempting to simply characterize this as literary bad manners,
which is how Lionel Trilling described F.R. Leavis's classic
attack on C.P. Snow's lectures on the two cultures. But even if
we think that, don't we also think, how refreshing, how – hit and
miss, maybe, but how – true? The curmudgeon, let's not forget,
is licensed to say the unspeakable, especially when what needs
saying is known but not publicly acknowledged by others. The
risks in *ad hominem* criticism are obvious; one invites personal
attacks in return.

Metcalf's ultimate defence rests, however, not on whether

he's right or wrong – although I have little doubt he considers his views to be the right ones – but on wit and style, on the ability to use words more elegantly, and therefore more memorably, than the 'pricks', 'hacks', newspaper reviewers, and second-rate writers he dismisses. Most of us produce copy with the simple intention of communicating an opinion, a body of information, and a handful of ideas. If our writing has any impact, if it is at all remembered, it's because of what we say and not how we say it. Metcalf's essays, by contrast, shift the emphasis from the former to the latter. The concern with ideas is still there but the style has been foregrounded to such an extent that there are occasions when we pay less attention to the substance than to the style. The style, if powerful enough, can deflect our focus from cognition to pleasure even though in our more sober moments we may agree with Shaftesbury that one of the tests of a truth lies in its ability to withstand ridicule. Unfortunately, if the ridicule takes a memorable enough form we may also recall it each time we bring a particular truth to mind. In the above passage, for example, Metcalf may or may not be unfair in describing Robin Mathews as 'the Ayatollah Khomeini of Canlit' but the phrase will probably linger in the minds of most of those who read the essay. (The same is true of his acidulous characterization of Michael Smith and Wayne Grady as 'Two buttocks of one bum' [KAP 181].[4])

But there's also a more positive, in the sense of less ambiguous, side to Metcalf's style. Consider the passage just quoted. Agree or disagree with it, you must admit that it's better written, more energetic, more various in its effects, more witty, more provocative, and simply more interesting than almost anything written on Canadian literature within the academy (don't overlook the 'almost'). It has several of Metcalf's typical gestures. There's the ridiculous biographical detail – Metcalfe / Metcalf / Metacalf – that lends immediacy and dramatic force to the larger argument; there are the opening and closing rhetorical questions spoken, one assumes, almost with contempt; the brief two-jab sentences puncturing the pretensions of a colonial press;

the telling remains of British idiom in 'Desperate stuff' with the noun carrying the residue of a profanity; and, finally, there's the overall structure of this section of the essay that creates the illusion of a narrative drive – 'But there is worse' – as St. George Metcalf is shown confronting greater and greater dangers in his encounters with the dragons of Canlit. Since it's Metcalf's essay St. George triumphs, the thrusts hit home, and the rhetorical gestures and flourishes linger in the reader's mind. I'll end this section with a few of my favourites.

On the English faculty at the University of Ottawa:

The faculty members seemed incurious; they struck me less as a community of scholars than as a gathering of soured accountants. (KAP 139)

On the 'cracker-barrel philosophy' in Alden Nowlan's later poetry:

At the end of that road lies the *Reader's Digest.* (KAP 122)

On nationalism and regionalism:

Defiant Canadian-ness is silly enough; defiant Saskatchewan-ness is pitiable. ('Curate's Egg' 37)

On bad poetry:

Poetry, *real* poetry, has been pretty much driven to the wall; it circulates in Canada rather like *samizdat* in Russia. There's a flood of excruciatingly *bad* poetry, of course, therapy stuff, thin gruel by intense young women, in the main, emanating from small presses like Fred Cogswell's Fiddlehead Poetry Books.... The wide circulation of all this *Cogswellerie* is cause for depression.... (KAP 52)

On W.D. Valgardson:

I recently re-read all his work when I was compiling an anthology for school children; I was appalled to discover that there was not a single story that was not suitable.
(KAP 160)

I hadn't realized until after having made the selection that each of these passages reveals a contestational stance or attitude: Metcalf against the University of Ottawa; Metcalf against nationalism and regionalism; Metcalf against bad poetry; Metcalf against the stories of W.D. Valgardson. In sum, Metcalf against Canada as it is because he makes demands on it that the country can't possibly fulfil. Since his demands and expectations have their origins in his experience and memories of a British society that no longer exists, Metcalf finds himself caught between past and present, and at home in neither.

It's the essential situation not only of the immigrant but also of the satirist and curmudgeon.

2. Metcalf as Flaubert

People don't sufficiently realize the trouble it takes to produce a well made sentence.
Gustave Flaubert[5]

STYLE, WHETHER IN CLOTHING or in prose, is Metcalf's way of distancing himself from the society that simultaneously arouses his wrath and stimulates his wit. The most exposed moments in his essays occur not when he rides off with Evelyn Waugh and Kingsley Amis to drive back the *canaille* of mass civilization but when he struts his own stuff in public, pointing to and annotating the local felicities of his style. The shock is almost as great as if Yves St. Laurent were to stop a fashion show to discuss the quality of the silk and the particular stitch or if an exceptionally supple and lubricious hooker were to pause to explain the contortions involved in her or his particular brand of *jouissance*. Metcalf doesn't actually say this but it's obvious that he divides the world not into sheep and goats or saved and damned but into those who have and know style (himself and a chosen few) and those who don't (Morley Callaghan, Canadian academics, and almost all Canadians before 1962 or so).

Metcalf admits that the argument on behalf of style is essentially a *parti pris* argument on behalf of John Metcalf and a small group of short story writers who function both as his culture club and, if ever necessary, his cover ('cover' as in 'run for cover' or 'cover me' or 'that's my cover'). Not a school or a movement, this group or band on the run includes Hugh Hood, Alice Munro, Mavis Gallant, Norman Levine, Clark Blaise, Audrey Thomas, and Leon Rooke. Not quite as distinguished as the gathering at Flaubert's Sunday afternoons in the mid-1870s, Metcalf's group could be said to represent an attitude to art similar to the one taken for granted by Flaubert's circle as well as, slightly later, by Mallarmé's. In Henry James's words,

> What was discussed in that little smoke-clouded room was chiefly questions of taste, questions of art and form, and the speakers, for the most part, were, in aesthetic matter, radicals of the deepest dye. It would have been late in the day to propose among them any discussion of the relation of art to morality, any question as to the degree in which a novel might or might not concern itself with the teaching of a lesson.... The only duty of a novel was to be well written; that merit included every other of which it was capable.[6]

Flaubert, in a sentence Metcalf would no doubt admire, makes a similar point in the passage I have used as the epigraph of this section. In that sentence are the roots of one branch of modernism, the branch that, according to Metcalf's re-reading of Canadian literary history, didn't reach Canada until the early 60s.

For Metcalf, Canadian modernism begins not with the

McGill Movement, not with the Montreal scene of the 1940s, not with *Contact*, and certainly not with the composite old pre-Edwardian fart Robertson Mac-Call'an: it begins somewhere in the sixties – probably 1962, the year Metcalf arrived in Canada – with a group of short story writers in whose work 'formal concerns' are more important than thematic ones (KAP 169). Metcalf develops the point in 'Editing the Best':

> It's probably a very dangerous analogy to make because painting and writing really cannot be compared but the changes in the short story in Canada over the last twenty years are not wildly unlike the changes in painting at a slightly earlier period. I'd suggest that the story pre-1962 could be compared with traditional representative painting and that the changes since have moved the story closer to an equivalent of abstraction. Though it's precisely there that the analogy collapses – for words have meanings. I don't mean to suggest by 'abstraction' that the modern story lacks immediate reference to the external world. Obviously not. I mean rather that formal concerns are becoming increasingly important....
>
> Our major story writers are Mavis Gallant, Norman Levine, Hugh Hood, Alice Munro, Leon Rooke, and Clark Blaise. Of these writers, Levine and Rooke are the ones most obviously concerned with rhetoric and form.
> (KAP 169)

From Metcalf's viewpoint, modernism is both a way of writing – Hemingway has it while Morley Callaghan doesn't – and of reading – the old New Critics, William Empson, and, I assume, the new French grammarians are in while F.R. Leavis and Lionel Trilling are out. Not surprisingly, then, Metcalf's witty, provocative, and slightly shrill essay 'The Curate's Egg' ends with a stirring call for a new formalism or *new* New Criticism. Arguing that the writers he admires produce stories that 'should be read with the same care that would be given to the reading of poems', he claims that most readers and critics lack a critical terminology that would allow them to respond properly to these 'new verse forms' ('Curate's Egg' 54). Metcalf concludes as follows:

> Let us say, for the sake of argument, that there are fifty such 'new verse forms', fifty such rhetorical devices, in common use by contemporary writers, and that not one of them has a commonly agreed upon name. Doesn't this argue that criticism is positively condemned to imprecision and vain groping? To inevitable misunderstanding?
>
> Because we lack the critical terminology, much of what goes on in stories remains misunderstood or undervalued or, worst of all, invisible. I have never seen any criticism anywhere which has the terminology to describe the technical achievements of a story by, say, Eudora Welty. Or, come to that, even of Hemingway. Criticism, it seems to me, lags light years behind the techniques which we are always extending and refining; no critical language exists to chart our explorations.
>
> Very little critical work has been done to identify the typical forms of beginnings, developments, or endings....
>
> I am suggesting, then, as humbly as I can, that the contemporary story is vitally rich and fiendishly subtle and that it is, for critics, *terra* which is close to *incognita*. ('Curate's Egg' 57-58)

This is Metcalf's Wittgensteinian moment: the limits of my critical language are the limits of my literary world. But are they? Can I not notice and respond to the solecisms, tortured syntax, and misspellings of the opening of Russell Hoban's *Riddley Walker* without having a more 'technical' name for what the devices and figures as a group represent? In what sense am I 'condemned' to 'inevitable misunderstanding' in reading Munro's *Lives of Girls and Women* if I don't have a term to describe the shift in narrative time in the book's final page? Or, similarly, will the lack of a more precise generic terminology prevent me from enjoying, understanding, teaching, and writing about the fictions of Hugh Hood, Norman Levine, and Michael Ondaatje, all of whom write fiction hinting at autobiography? Finally, who will benefit if I invent a term to describe Mavis Gallant's syntactical and semantic mannerism of writing sentences that are almost but not quite epigrammatic? To return to Metcalf's painting analogy: it may be fascinating for a handful of connoisseurs to debate why some brushstrokes in a certain painting by Camille Pissaro are applied from an unusual direction and what the technique should be called, but that's definitely not why most of us stand entranced before *Les Toits Rouges*. Granted that the brushstrokes can be said to *be* the painting, nevertheless, what the painting ultimately *is* for the viewer transcends any strictly formal analysis of technique.

Metcalf's various caveats as well as the general canniness of his arguments make it clear that he realizes this. The comment quoted earlier in which he reminds us that he's not insisting that 'the modern story lacks immediate reference to the external world' is just one of many similar qualifications. And yet the overall rhetorical and formal stress is in the other direction. An interview in 1981, for example, sets up an opposition between 'clumsy, laborious, repetitive, and unsubtle' D.H. Lawrence and that 'tremendous craftsman' Evelyn Waugh who 'turned in wonderful verbal performances of supreme elegance' and whose use of 'the semi-colon' Metcalf finds admirable and worthy of study. Lawrence is also rejected because '[h]e was an obsessive *ideas* man' (KAP 7). Like those other duffers, George Eliot, Tolstoy, and Dostoevsky (my examples, not Metcalf's), he thought he had something to say about the world, or about what Faulkner, in the foreword to *The Mansion,* called 'the human heart and its dilemma'.[7] Waugh, by contrast, thought of writing 'not as investigation of character but as an exercise in the use of language'. Thus '[a]ny moron can tell you what a Waugh novel is "about". Unimportant. What *is* important is how the work is *performed*' (KAP 6). Comments like these create the impression that at some point Metcalf will raise the banner for post-modernism. Instead, though not surprisingly for someone so attached to the British tradition of comic writing, he stops far short with the modernism of the Canadian sixties. After citing Waugh's hilarious comment that James Joyce went mad to please the Americans, he states the following:

> I don't think the 'representational', if I can say that, is played out.... I don't *like* reading all that George Bowering stuff. Although my primary loyalties are to style, I like the artifice and rhetoric to connect me to a real world, actual or imagined. The sort of stuff that George is always nattering on about – reflexive fiction or whatever they call it – is like a sort of literary Rubik's Cube. (KAP 5)

In 'Telling Tales' he mentions – in a simile borrowed from Joyce Cary – that he 'always felt that much "experimental" writing was rather like farting "Annie Laurie" through a keyhole though not as demanding' (KAP 78).

So where does that leave us? Or rather where does that leave Metcalf? Is he simply a belated new critic over-stating the case for technique or artifice in a neo-colonial situation where readers don't realize that *'Reading a story is a purely literary activity'* ('Curate's Egg' 52)? Is he correct in dismissing much of what passed for literature in Canada before 1950 as 'rubbish'? Are his attacks on nationalism and chauvinism in Canadian culture the natural and necessary reaction to the fervour of the past three decades? The answer to all of these questions is an undoubted yes, but we need to take one further item into account. Let's not forget that Metcalf is not just a critic but a *writer-critic* who also happened to be an immigrant. I mention the fact of his immigration not in order to call into question his Canadian-ness but to offer a potential explanation for his attempt to rewrite the Canadian canon: Metcalf, as I will argue below, is simply trying to fashion a Canadian tradition in which he will have a place. I make the point about Metcalf being a writer-critic because it seems to me that every writer since Horace who has turned his attention to criticism has done so for the following reasons: to argue the case for his own work, to squeeze it into the canon (for Metcalf's fiction this is somewhere between Wodehouse and Waugh at one end and Gallant, Hood, and Munro at the other), to teach his readers how to read him, and, finally, to offer a tacit evaluation of his own work (just look at the company Metcalf keeps).

Metcalf's problematic relationship to literary tradition seems to me to underlie, in part, his emphasis on style and on a criticism that focuses almost exclusively on style, form, and rhetoric. One of the more obvious consequences of a predominantly 'practical' or textual or rhetorical criticism is that it eliminates most, perhaps all, of the distinctions that would allow us to discuss texts either historically or within national traditions. Approached in this way all literature is extra-territorial. The only basis on which a group of books could then be classified as English or Canadian or Australian would be political or geographical. (Obviously the argument would take a different form if we were dealing with a literature like Czech or French that is defined *a priori* by a unique language.) I'm not suggesting, however, that a content-oriented or thematic criticism is the alternative – that way lie Moss and madness. I simply want to make it clear that if we follow some of Metcalf's suggestions or those of critics who tempt us with Barthesian *jouissance* or Derridean deconstruction then we are pulling the theoretical rug out from under Canadian studies constituted as a separate branch of English studies. That may or may not be a bad thing. If nothing else it would force us to re-examine more closely what our actual field of study is and how it relates to other areas of the discipline. But if we agree that our major texts, those which constitute or determine our field of study, are written in a modern or international style and if we take it for granted that '*il n'y a pas de hors-texte*'[8] then we have no theoretical basis on which to constitute a canon that is specifically Canadian – unless we want to do it on the basis of place of publication. We may agree with Metcalf's figure that 'Canadian writing is only a weak current in a strong English-language river' ('Curate's Egg' 40) but if we follow his argument we will have no way of distinguishing the one from the other.

Similarly, in dismissing 'most Canadian writing up until 1950' as 'rubbish' (KAP 58) and by characterizing the best work since about 1962 as modern or international in style Metcalf, consciously or unconsciously, leaves the Canadian writer and critic without a Canadian tradition. Whether such a tradition exists as something more than a body of texts published over a number of years in a particular place is, of course, a moot point. A strongly defined national literary tradition is probably only possible in countries with indigenous languages and lengthy histories that reached regional or national consciousness prior to the 1848 revolutions. A colony that became a dominion in 1867 and achieved real nationhood only the better part of a century later will experience the idea of a tradition differently than an established European nation. The differences may be so great that we may feel the need for a new word, or a conceptualization of the problem far more complex than any we have so far been offered.

Yet Metcalf's tacit if radical dismantling of the rickety scaffolding of a Canadian tradition ultimately affects only those writers like Al Purdy, Margaret Laurence, Rudy Wiebe, and Margaret Atwood who see themselves as having a place in it. His wrecking ball doesn't touch those who either don't think about it – Mordecai Richler, Norman Levine, and Mavis Gallant – or whose roots are elsewhere – Leon Rooke, Audrey Thomas, Michael Ondaatje, and, surprise, surprise, John Metcalf. This doesn't mean, however, that Metcalf himself is left without a tradition. Even the most cursory reading of his non-fiction makes it obvious that he's a Canadian writer and editor who thinks of his fiction as related to two groups: the first is the group of Canadian short story writers I mentioned near the beginning of this section; the second consists of the line of the great English humorists from Peacock, through Wodehouse and Waugh, to Kingsley

Amis and Beryl Bainbridge (KAP 6). 'Noddy and Big Ears Meet Malvolio', his memoir of his childhood reading, is a sentimental evocation of another part of the same terrain (Orwell, Greene, and Bertie Wooster would have been at home with Metcalf's books).

Metcalf's comments, from the 1981 interview, on his uneasy relationships with Canada and England deserve quotation:

> One writes about where one lives. I happen to live in Canada. I *have* been writing about Canada from the viewpoint of being an immigrant to this country and I get considerable mileage out of the comic and serious contrasts between Canada and Europe. But it's all emotionally complicated. Canada is my home. Soon, I'll have lived here more than half my life. Yet, at the same time, I'm still something of a stranger. But it's *also* true that I feel even more of a stranger in England. I'm caught between two worlds. And one of them exists only in memory – is maybe even partially invented. It isn't difficult to invent England.
>
> You see, the England of my childhood which I remember so richly is totally gone. *That* world had its links clearly and visibly back into the mists of the English past. The Second World War ended so much. In its aftermath, the past was obliterated. Physically, socially – in every way. And then TV finished the job off. (KAP 3)

Perhaps Metcalf was omitted from *The Penguin Book of Canadian Short Stories* because with his background – his 'traditions' – he couldn't be fitted into the line of development that extends from 'the Letter to the Editor' through the '*Daily Stump and Stone Picker*' to the present (KAP 150)? Whatever the case, Metcalf's revisionist recasting of the idea of a national literary tradition, with the short story as its focus, makes room for writers like himself who weren't nurtured on *Wacousta* and back issues of the *Canadian Forum*. Not coincidentally, most of the writers he admires have as complicated a relationship with tradition as he does.

Certainly Metcalf is at his most involved and acidulous when discussing the Canadian short story. Most of the threads of his polemics are involved with it: the insensitivity of critics, the lack of a literate audience, the idea of a Canadian tradition, modernism, the sins of the academy. Having dedicated two decades to the writing and editing of stories Metcalf tends to look upon the short story much in the same proprietary way that Norman Mailer regards boxing or Eugene Forsey the Canadian constitution. A crucial part of his championing of the 'modern' story involves the denigration of those stories that strike him as spuriously modern. In Canada that means Morley Callaghan and Hugh Garner. Garner he treats as almost beneath contempt, referring at one point to his 'mindless *oeuvre*' (KAP 150). Callaghan is one of his *bêtes noires* and is trotted out whenever he needs an example of the backwardness of Canadian fiction or the insensitivity of Canadian critics. His disdain for Callaghan is extended on the basis of a sort of guilt by association to critics who have written approvingly of the grand old man of Canadian letters. Yet Metcalf's overall argument – or, at least, what I take to be the sub-text of his argument – needs Callaghan almost as much as his attack on Canadian taste needs the University of Ottawa, John Moss, Robin Mathews, and Wayne Grady. If Metcalf can convince us that Callaghan is a second-rate writer, he can simultaneously demonstrate the incompetence of our reviewers and critics since for two generations or more they have accepted and spread the view that Callaghan is either our Hemingway (the claim made implicitly by Callaghan himself in *That Summer in Paris*[9]) or our Turgenev or Chekhov (Edmund Wilson's bizarre suggestion in *O Canada*[10]). The rejection of Callaghan is also, of course, a clearing away of some of the deadwood of the past that would make an argument for a Canadian tradition possible. Instead of being seen as an early modernist and essential precursor, Callaghan is viewed like the eccentric uncle whose scribblings have been treated too fondly for far too long. MacLennan, against whose old-fashioned and long-winded novels an equally strong case could be made, is spared because he didn't trespass onto the short story preserve.

With the dead-wood cleared away, the work of revision can begin. The following sentences from 'Editing the Best' and 'The Curate's Egg' indicate its nature:

> If forced to generalities, I'd say that the strongest genre in Canada is the short story and the weakest the novel. It would not be realistic to hope for more than one major poet in any fifty year period. In any country. Our two most important poets are Irving Layton and John Newlove but it's far too early to assess their achievement. I suspect that the idea of a 'major poet' – one who changes our emotional landscape and recharges our language – is now an historical concept; impact requires audience and poetry has become dangerously marginal. The sensibility and manner of our best story writers is basically poetic and it may well be that there is something about our times that prompts people who might once have written poetry to write prose instead. (KAP 167)

> ... some of our contemporary writers offer a feast as sumptuous as any. Hugh Hood, Alice Munro, Norman Levine, Clark Blaise, Mavis Gallant, Leon Rooke, Audrey Thomas, and a new writer probably unknown to you, Keath Fraser.... ('Curate's Egg' 58)

The ghost in the second quotation is, of course, Metcalf, whose best fiction is as interesting as the stories of most of the writers named – Munro and Gallant are in a class by themselves. At the core of Metcalf's argument are the assertions that, one, the best work in Canadian literature is being done in the story and, two, a particular body of work in the short story can stand comparison with the best writing being done in English elsewhere. One can agree with both of these propositions yet suspect that Metcalf is ultimately asserting much less than he seems to be because the 'feast' offered by Canada consists solely of short stories; the feast from elsewhere includes the novel (Naipaul, Gordimer, Mailer, Bellow, Rushdie, Pynchon). Perhaps what leaves me uneasy is not the echo of the old line, 'Great things are beginning to be done in Canada', but that Metcalf is making large claims on behalf of Canadian literature based on what is essentially a minor or secondary form. Yes, we all know that it is just as difficult to write a perfect short story as it is to write *Anna Karenina* or *The Rainbow* and that it is philistine to be impressed by the scope, ambition, and bulk of the novel. But it's the inescapable fact of our literary experience that, as Frank Kermode once put it, 'in our phase of civility, the novel is the central form of literary art'.[11] The short story writer resembles the miniaturist in painting or the composer specializing in preludes or the featherweight boxer: the interesting action is elsewhere. Not unexpectedly, the only time that we see major claims being made for writers like Mansfield or Welty and the inevitable handful of others is in essays like Metcalf's where a *parti pris* critic or writer is asserting the importance of the sub-genre. Everyone else takes it for granted that a great writer can throw off a story between chapters of a novel. Obviously I exaggerate, but I can't help thinking of Tolstoy, James, Lawrence, Faulkner, and Hemingway, who move easily between the two forms. Rudy Wiebe – Metcalf's most obvious blind spot – Hugh Hood, and Jack Hodgins are the Canadian examples that come to mind.

There's something more. It has to do with my calling the short story a minor form, and I can put it best by citing Pasternak's comment that we read Tolstoy and Dostoevsky 'because they had something to say.'[12] In the sense of the phrase intended by Pasternak, most short story writers have nothing to say, and we don't expect it of them any more than we expect an epic poem from a lyric poet. The story writer is simply constrained by the limits of his form. Pasternak's 'something to say' involves a world view, 'ideas', and a vision of human destiny of such grandeur and profundity that only the novel, the most elastic of our genres, can provide an adequate vehicle for it. The short story, by contrast, usually gives local insights, visionary moments, epiphanies; instead of a world, a situation. No wonder, then, that Metcalf wants to turn our attention to style and form; he is emphasizing the story's one undoubted strength: its scope may be limited but its world is perfectly organized. No wonder, also, that if we apply Metcalf's distorting view of fiction to the novel, Evelyn Waugh, that brilliant writer but second-rank novelist, is preferred to a giant like Lawrence.

The Canadian short story may or may not be as good as Metcalf claims. And some, I assume, would be willing to challenge the view that the best work in Canadian literature in the past three decades has been done in short fiction. These arguments can be pursued elsewhere. All that is important here is my impression that Metcalf *must* offer a high valuation of short fiction – the fiction he excels in – if he is to recast the Canadian tradition in such a way that he will have a place in it. Thus those readers of 'Without an "E"' who heard an immigrant voice and a note of self-interest were right but for the wrong reasons. If there's an element of self-interest here, it's of the same kind that we see in Pound and Eliot's re-reading of English poetry from the perspective of their own early work. The writer-critic, as I mentioned earlier, almost always attempts to restructure the canon in order to make it accommodate his own writing and, incidentally, to assert the primacy or superiority of his genre. Thus even an episode as insignificant as Metcalf's disagreement with Wayne Grady and Grady's editing of *The Penguin Book of Canadian Short Stories* needs to be seen from this perspective. The argument is over many things including the quality of Grady's book-reviewing – 'a malicious incompetent' (KAP 177) says Metcalf – but ultimately it's a territorial dispute over control of the Canadian short story and Metcalf's place in it. By leaving Metcalf out of the Penguin anthology, Grady effectively put a local check to Metcalf's ambitious revisionism in the bush garden.

Revisionism always takes place on the basis of selective memory and subjective predilections. But *Kicking Against the Pricks* goes one further in insisting on a revaluation based on a cultural forgetting that will clear the space for a *new* internationally-oriented tradition in fiction and in criticism. Not surprisingly, Metcalf's stories figure in the former and *Kicking Against the Pricks* is one of the essential texts of the latter.

Postscript: January 1989

1. 'Some Kicks Against the Prick' was written over four years ago between chapters of a book on Josef Skvorecky's fiction I was working on at the time. The essay began as a response to John Metcalf's various comments on the short story but developed, in a slightly broken-backed way, into what still seems to me a relatively admiring reading of Metcalf's criticism. And although Metcalf refers to it in 'Dear Sam' as 'rudely titled', I thought of it then as both homage and *hommage* to a writer I admired for his style, panache, and critical intelligence. At worst, I thought of my disagreements with him as a family quarrel. Therefore I must admit to being slightly baffled by Metcalf's failure to see just how admiring a piece of work this essay really is. Surely one of the allusions in the title playfully suggests as much: 'And [Saul] said, Who art thou, Lord? And the Lord said, I am Jesus whom thou persecutest; it is hard for thee to kick against the pricks.'[13]

2. As far as I can tell, Metcalf sees two major points of disagreement between us. The first, dealt with in *What Is A Canadian Literature?*, concerns tradition; the second, discussed in 'Dear Sam', concerns the relationship between style and theme or between form and content.

On the question of tradition, I think Metcalf misrepresents my views. In his eagerness to find a replacement for Robin Mathews – who served as the menacing representative of a narrow, chauvinistic, nationalistic attitude to literature in *Kicking Against the Pricks* – Metcalf misinterprets what I actually write in my essay. The lengthy passage quoted in the opening pages of *What Is A Canadian Literature?* is not a statement of my views on tradition or the Canadian tradition in literature. It is a *description* of what a more nationally and historically oriented alternative to Metcalf's international definition would look like. The passage deliberately raises questions and points to problems.

If pressed to develop the argument further, I would insist that Metcalf's view of a Canadian literary tradition is, in its own way, as limited as the narrowly nationalistic version he attacks. Any description of a Canadian tradition that leaves out lines of influence running from Susanna Moodie to Margaret Atwood, from *The Jesuit Relations* to E.J. Pratt's *Brébeuf and His Brethren* and to Brian Moore's *Black Robe,* from Sinclair Ross to Margaret Laurence and to Rudy Wiebe, from the popular culture of the twenties, thirties, and forties to the novels of Hugh Hood – such an account will be as useful and reliable on Canadian literature as Soviet encyclopedias of the 1950s were on the heroes of the Revolution.

'Some Kicks Against the Prick', I want to repeat, offers two descriptions of a Canadian tradition – Metcalf's and the one summarized in the preceding paragraph. Any serious discussion of the Canadian tradition in literature will need to include both. (The question becomes even more complicated as we try to offer a view of a 'Canadian tradition' that includes writers like Rohinton Mistry and Neil Bissoondath.) While Metcalf and I seem to agree that most of the writing in this country before 1960 isn't particularly interesting, I nevertheless see it as historically important and, on occasion, even influential, whereas he doesn't. The evidence of the *Literary History of Canada* and *The Oxford Companion to Canadian Literature* doesn't impress him because he approaches the work of his Canadian predecessors on the lookout for what he can use. In other words, Metcalf approaches tradition from the point of view of a practising writer, and the only work of the past that catches his attention is the writing still alive – because influential – in the work of important contemporaries.

I emphasize 'important' because Metcalf's dismissal or neglect of historically important second-rate writers seems to me related to his general emphasis on the need for evaluation and standards in criticism. He recognizes rightly that academic critics dealing with Canadian literature often forget that a writer may be historically important – John Richardson or Isabella Valancy Crawford – and yet not worth reading except for strictly historical reasons. (Only a sadist would recommend Crawford to someone who loves poetry.) Unlike Metcalf, however, I think that literary history and evaluative criticism can cohabit.

3. Discussing my use of Boris Pasternak's comment that such figures as Tolstoy and Dostoevsky were great writers 'because they had something to say', Metcalf claims in 'Dear Sam' that this, together with my attitude to D.H. Lawrence and Rudy Wiebe, shows that I separate style and theme or form and content. This is a slippery area. I'm willing to concede at the outset that I don't value style to the extent that Metcalf does. We agree that Waugh writes very well indeed, but while Waugh's novels send Metcalf into paroxysms of praise, I find them mildly amusing and minor. David Lodge's comment in *The Novelist at the Crossroads* that Waugh 'brought the minor novel to its peak of perfection'[14] seems to me just.

The dancer may be inseparable from the dance, but when the dancing is fiction then style is a means to an end or embodies an end which is something other than just style. It is a commonplace that poetry dances but prose walks: it has a goal or object or end. We both begin with words and style, but Metcalf seems content to stay there and I am not. He discusses fiction as if it were abstract art where style is everything. All of this, incidentally, doesn't mean that I agree with Philip Larkin who once said that 'Form holds little interest for me. Content is everything.'[15]

One of the paradoxes of fiction is that a writer can produce a good novel and yet be occasionally plodding, clumsy, awkward, ponderous, tin-eared, etc. Turgenev, for example, is a finer stylist than Dostoevsky and he certainly never embarrasses the reader with the out-of-control melodrama frequently found in *The Possessed* or *The Brothers Karamazov*, yet there's no doubt which of the two is the greater writer. As Pasternak recognized, Dostoevsky 'had something to say'. And more often than not, of course, he said it well. Like Pasternak, in other words, I'm not praising just content. Pasternak, after all, refers to Tolstoy and Dostoevsky not Chernyshevsky (the author of *What Is To Be Done?*, the most influential bad novel of the nineteenth century); I cite Lawrence and Wiebe not Mazo de la Roche.

On the question of the short story, I acknowledge the artistry and vision of the examples Metcalf cites in 'Dear Sam' but I still have the strong impression that even the best short story (like the one-act play, the short opera, the sketch, and the *maquette*) is a slighter, less significant piece of work than the first-rate novel. This whole argument may be based on a category error originating with me: some people admire sprinters; others, milers. Nevertheless, were I a betting man I would bet that plodding, awkward, and unstylish Theodore Dreiser will be read a century from now while most of our favourite short story writers will be little more than brief entries in literary histories.

As for the quotations from Lawrence and Wiebe in 'Dear Sam', I could easily quote counter-examples from *The Rainbow* and *The Blue Mountains of China* in which the style is everything Metcalf demands. But to be candid, I *am* willing to forgive a great deal in a writer who, for whatever reason, speaks to me.

4. Finally, I must admit being completely mystified by Alice Munro's statement – quoted approvingly by Metcalf in 'Dear Sam' – that she 'can start reading [stories] anywhere; from beginning to end, from end to beginning, from any point in between in either direction'.[16] With all due respect to both writers, there seems to me something so obviously wrong in this attitude that I can only conclude they're pulling my leg.

NOTES

1   Peter Handke, *A Moment of True Feeling*, trans. Ralph Manheim (New York: Farrar, Straus and Giroux, 1977) 8.

2   My essay will refer to the two following texts: *Kicking Against the Pricks* (Downsview, ON: ECW, 1982; 2nd ed., Guelph, ON: Red Kite, 1986) and 'The Curate's Egg', *Essays on Canadian Writing* 30 (1984-85): 35-59. All references will be incorporated into the body of this essay, with *Kicking Against the Pricks* abbreviated to KAP and 'The Curate's Egg' to 'Curate's Egg'.

3   Quoted by Josef Skvorecky in *The Engineer of Human Souls*, trans. Paul Wilson (Toronto: Lester & Orpen Dennys, 1984) 292.

4   The comment was originally made by T. Sturge Moore with reference to G.K. Chesterton and Hilaire Belloc as Metcalf acknowledges.

5   I quote from memory.

6   Quoted by Francis Steegmuller in *The Letters of Gustave Flaubert 1857-1880*, selected, edited, and translated by Francis Steegmuller (Cambridge, MA: Harvard UP, 1982) 224-25.

7   William Faulkner, foreword, *The Mansion* (1959; New York: Vintage, 1965) n. pag.

8   Jacques Derrida, *Of Grammatology*, trans. Gayatri Chakravorty Spivak (Baltimore, MD: The Johns Hopkins UP, 1976) 158.

9   See Morley Callaghan, *That Summer in Paris: Memories of Tangled Friendships with Hemingway, Fitzgerald and Some Others* (Toronto: Macmillan, 1963).

10   See Edmund Wilson, 'Morley Callaghan of Toronto', *O Canada: An American's Notes on Canadian Culture* (New York: Farrar, Straus and Giroux, 1964) 21.

11   Frank Kermode, *The Sense of an Ending: Studies in the Theory of Fiction* (New York: Oxford UP, 1967) 128.

12   Boris Pasternak, *My Sister, Life and Other Poems*, ed. and with texts by Olga Andreyev Carlisle (New York: Harcourt Brace Jovanovich, 1976) 113. The comment comes in a conversation with Olga Carlisle which is printed as an appendix to Pasternak's collection of poems.

The full sentence reads as follows: 'The voices of those writers sounded like thunder because they had something to say.' Pasternak is referring to Dostoevsky, Tolstoy, and Blok.

13 Acts 9.5.

14 David Lodge, *The Novelist at the Crossroads and Other Essays on Fiction and Criticism* (Ithaca, NY: Cornell UP, 1971) 25.

15 Philip Larkin, as quoted in David Lodge, *The Modes of Modern Writing: Metaphor, Metonymy, and the Typology of Modern Literature* (Ithaca, NY: Cornell UP, 1977) 214.

16 Alice Munro, 'What Is Real?', *Making It New: Contemporary Canadian Stories*, ed. John Metcalf (Toronto: Methuen, 1982) 224.

Dear Sam

... I wonder how much of the vilification modern British philosophy encounters comes from its tendency to resist the act of paraphrase, to remain obdurately philosophical in the face of attempts to boil off its 'technique' and reduce it to a series of assertions constituting a 'world view'. But that is not my battle. Literature is, and the situation there is more serious, for this, as no other, is a field in which any fool can have an opinion. Nearly any fool, plus many non-fools in their weaker, more fatigued, less attentive moments, would rather read a book as a purée of trends and attitudes than as a work of art having its own unique, unparaphrasable qualities. And here comes my chance to do justice to *Scrutiny* by observing that at any rate it fought hard against this kind of Philistinism, and that it represented the only important body of opinion on that side of the fight.

Any decent writer sees his first concern as the rendering of what he takes to be permanent in human nature, and this holds true no matter how 'contemporary' his material. Now and again he may feel – we should perhaps think less of him if he did not ever feel – that there are some political causes too vast or urgent to be subordinated to mere literature, and will allow one or other such to determine the shape of what he writes. But by doing so he will have been guilty of betrayal. He will have accelerated the arrival of the day on which it is generally agreed that a novel or a poem or a play is no more than a system of generalizations orchestrated in terms of plot and diction and situation and the rest; the day, in other words, on which the novel, the poem, and the play cease to exist....

Kingsley Amis, 'Lone Voices', in his *What Became of Jane Austen? and Other Questions*

One thing I hold as certain, that a writer, if he is to develop, must concern himself more and more with Style. He cannot hope to interest the majority of his readers in his progress. It is his own interest that is at stake. Style alone can keep him from being bored with his own work. In youth high spirits carry one over a book or two. The world is full of discoveries that demand expression. Later a writer must face the choice of becoming an artist or a prophet. He can shut himself up at his desk and selfishly seek pleasure in the perfecting of his own skill or he can pace about, dictating dooms and exhortations on the topics of the day. The recluse at the desk has a bare chance of giving abiding pleasure to others; the publicist has none at all.

Evelyn Waugh, 'Literary Style in England and America', in his *A Little Order*

DEAR SAM: This essay or 'discourse', as I understand you lot call bits of writing these days, started out – as befits a man of my advancing years – in a style both formal and mildly pompous, but I found I was boring myself; it seemed impossibly strained and rhetorical to continue referring to you as 'Professor Solecki' – especially so when in real life, as it were, we call each other Sam and John – and I must also confess that I've discovered I'm beginning to find polemics tiresome. I intend retiring the putty nose and bladder-on-a-stick. No more carping, no more capering, no more cap and bells. This essay seeks a new tone and a new direction.

Our debate began with my writing *Kicking Against the Pricks* and 'The Curate's Egg' and your attacking aspects of them in your rudely titled essay 'Some Kicks Against the Prick: John Metcalf in His Essays'. This relatively brief essay of yours seemed to me so *densely* wrong-headed that it provoked me to a 104-page book in reply. I hope that *What Is A Canadian Literature?* will help to focus for us the meaning of the word 'tradition' when we apply it to writing in Canada. Many might consider 104 pages of reply more than enough but 'Some Kicks Against the Prick' contained other serious matters not yet touched upon which caused the eyebrow to rise. I refer, of course, to your appalling remarks on the short story as a genre.

Here's what you said:

At the core of Metcalf's argument are the assertions that,

one, the best work in Canadian literature is being done in the story and, two, a particular body of work in the short story can stand comparison with the best writing being done in English elsewhere. One can agree with both of these propositions yet suspect that Metcalf is ultimately asserting much less than he seems to be because the 'feast' offered by Canada consists solely of short stories; the feast from elsewhere includes the novel (Naipaul, .Gordimer, Mailer, Bellow, Rushdie, Pynchon). Perhaps what leaves me uneasy is not the echo of the old line, 'Great things are beginning to be done in Canada', but that Metcalf is making large claims on behalf of Canadian literature based on what is essentially a minor or secondary form. Yes, we all know that it is just as difficult to write a perfect short story as it is to write *Anna Karenina* or *The Rainbow* and that it is philistine to be impressed by the scope, ambition, and bulk of the novel. But it's the inescapable fact of our literary experience that, as Frank Kermode once put it, 'in our phase of civility, the novel is the central form of literary art'. The short story writer resembles the miniaturist in painting or the composer specializing in preludes or the feather-weight boxer: the interesting action is elsewhere. Not unexpectedly, the only time that we see major claims being made for writers like Mansfield or Welty and the inevitable handful of others is in essays like Metcalf's where a *parti pris* critic or writer is asserting the importance of the sub-genre. Everyone else takes it for granted that a great writer can throw off a story between chapters of a novel. Obviously I exaggerate, but I can't help thinking of Tolstoy, James, Lawrence, Faulkner, and Hemingway, who move easily between the two forms. Rudy Wiebe – Metcalf's most obvious blind spot – Hugh Hood, and Jack Hodgins are the Canadian examples that come to mind.

There's something more. It has to do with my calling the short story a minor form, and I can put it best by citing Pasternak's comment that we read Tolstoy and Dostoevsky 'because they had something to say'. In the sense of the phrase intended by Pasternak, most short story writers have nothing to say, and we don't expect it of them any more than we expect an epic poem from a lyric poet. The story writer is simply constrained by the limits of his form. Pasternak's 'something to say' involves a world view, 'ideas', and a vision of human destiny of such grandeur and profundity that only the novel, the most elastic of our genres, can provide an adequate vehicle for it. The short story, by contrast, usually gives local insights, visionary moments, epiphanies; instead of a world, a situation. No wonder, then, that Metcalf wants to turn our attention to style and form; he is emphasizing the story's one undoubted strength: its scope may be limited but its world is perfectly organized. No wonder, also, that if we apply Metcalf's distorting view of fiction to the novel, Evelyn Waugh, that brilliant writer but second-rank novelist, is preferred to a giant like Lawrence.

The Canadian short story may or may not be as good as Metcalf claims. And some, I assume, would be willing to challenge the view that the best work in Canadian literature in the past three decades has been done in short fiction. These arguments can be pursued elsewhere. All that is important here is my impression that Metcalf *must* offer a high valuation of short fiction – the fiction he excels in – if he is to recast the Canadian tradition in such a way that he will have a place in it.

Well!
'Featherweights' forsooth!
Some of these remarks and attitudes, Sam, occasioned in me much the same depths of pain as those felt by Jeeves when the unsupervised Bertie came home from a holiday on the Riviera sporting a white cummerbund.

A sharp intake of the breath, if you know what I mean.

But I must remember that I have forsworn buffoonery and comic effects.

This lengthy quotation from 'Some Kicks Against the Prick' is less an example of reasoned argument, it seems to me, than it is a display of a certain kind of thinking and feeling, a certain kind of temperament. The words 'a difference of opinion' are inadequate to describe the differences between us; the differences between us are profound. We're on opposite sides of one of the great and natural human divides – neat people and untidy people, morning people and night people, Big Endians and Little Endians, those who save the best till last and those who eat the best bits first.

Our attitudes represent the opposing poles of literary response; I'd like to explore the whys and hows of these polar differences between us because while they're deeply personal they're also representative and should therefore be of general interest.

My approach to all this will be wayward and meandering – snapshots, memories, quotations. I will need your patience.

A COUPLE OF YEARS AGO, exhausted by Culture, I was sitting in the Piazza della Signoria sipping a beer and watching the girls walk by. Tourists were busily clicking away at the array of sculptures outside the Palazzo Vecchio, Hercules and David, that sort of thing, impossibly huge and improbably muscled. Standing in the shadow of the copy of Michelangelo's *David* and regarding it with a face so impassive it made me grin was a small besuited Japanese tourist. I don't know what *he* was thinking but *I* was thinking how much more deeply moving and artistic for me was the slightest work by Hokusai or Hiroshige.

Similarly, I was in Assisi this year looking at the Giotto and Cimabue frescoes. I recognized their importance in the Development of Western Art and all that sort of thing, and the colours are lovely still, and some of the panels are whimsically charming, but over lunch I found myself thinking about a watercolour I'd seen a couple of weeks earlier in the Ashmolean Museum in Oxford, a watercolour by Ling Feng-Mien called *Java Sparrows on a Wisteria Bough.*

I realize that switching from literature to visual art is suicidally dangerous in arguments such as these and I realize that in a moment I may be ascribing to Sam tastes he doesn't possess but I suspect that there is an interesting pattern here and that the references to visual art will help to reveal it. I suspect that Sam would genuinely *like* Michelangelo's *David* and the Giotto frescoes and the Sistine Chapel while my response would be more dutiful; I suspect too that my deep and genuine pleasure in a bronze door knob, say, in St. Peter's would strike him as perverse, eccentric, or provocative. I know I have this effect on some people. In Slovenia a couple of years ago I positively infuriated a friend when I enthused in a medieval castle not over the keep, dungeons, chapel, or magnificent view but over the design and balance of the wrought-iron locks and latches on the doors, latches which in the north of England dialect of my childhood were called 'snecks', a lovely word that has not been in my mind for forty years or more.

What exactly do I mean by these confessions?

Am I agreeing with Sam's dismissal of us as 'miniaturists'? Am I suggesting that story writers prefer the small, the intimate, the domestic? Are story writers marked as some old-fashioned critics once claimed by a 'feminine sensibility'? Are we drawn naturally to the smaller canvas, to sensitive portraits of hearth and home?

No, that's not at all what I'm getting at.

What is it that Michelangelo's Sistine Chapel frescoes and *David* have that Ling Feng-Mien's *Java Sparrows on a Wisteria Bough* does not? Simply, Michelangelo's work expresses ideas while Ling Feng-Mien's doesn't. *David* is not simply a representation of a nude male. Nor is it simply a representation of a biblical hero. *David* – while it is both male nude and hero – is also an expression of Renaissance thought and feeling about man's place and importance in the universe. The sculpture, to quote Sam quoting Pasternak, has 'something to say'.

And it is this 'having something to say' that is at the root of the disagreements between us. All literature, of course, has something to say because it isn't paint and because words have meanings. But Sam means something more specific.

Let me re-quote him:

> Pasternak's 'something to say' involves a world view, 'ideas', and a vision of human destiny of such grandeur and profundity that only the novel, the most elastic of our genres, can provide an adequate vehicle for it.

How, then, are we to approach and evaluate Ling Feng-Mien's *Java Sparrows on a Wisteria Bough* which expresses nothing but the wash of colour and the sumptuousness of *sumi* ink? How are we to approach and understand the stories of Eudora Welty which express a great deal but scarcely 'a world view' in the Pasternakian sense?

This comparison between writing and painting is illogical and unfair, of course, but usefully suggestive.

Just in passing. I'd say that Pasternak always struck me as a nineteenth-century writer and Russia from what I understand of it as a country more of the nineteenth century still than of the twentieth. It also seems to me that what Sam wants literature to do and the way he wants literature to do it are nineteenth-century requirements. Much modern writing – perhaps most of it – has questioned or denied the very idea of 'a world view' and such 'visions of human destiny' as we've been given have been marked by gloom rather than grandeur. A figure more typical of the twentieth century than Pasternak is Woody Allen.

Even the asking of The Big Questions has become in Woody Allen's movies the staple of comedy. *Angst* itself is Allen's *shtick*. We laugh at Allen because only a clown now believes in the possibility of answers. In a recent movie, *Hannah and Her Sisters*,

Allen's typical *nebbish* figure returns home to his Jewish mother and father and announces that because he needs something to believe in he is going to become a Christian. His mother promptly locks herself in the bathroom and refuses to come out.

Woody Allen addresses the locked door.

'If there's a God,' he says, 'why is there so much evil in the world? Just on a simplistic level, why were there Nazis?'

The mother's voice calls to the father: 'Tell him, Max.'

And Max says: 'How the hell do I know why there were Nazis? I don't know how the can-opener works.'

Well, it struck a chord with me.

And it makes a point.

But the really interesting part of Sam's sentence about 'a world view' is this: 'only the novel, the most elastic of our genres, can provide an adequate vehicle for it'.

'An adequate vehicle'.

Think of the implications of those words. And they are not simply a slip of the tongue, as it were. Elsewhere in the text of 'Some Kicks Against the Prick' Sam actually spells out what he here implies:

> Metcalf's ultimate defence rests, however, not on whether he's right or wrong – although I have little doubt he considers his views to be the right ones – but on wit and style, on the ability to use words more elegantly, and therefore more memorably, than the 'pricks', 'hacks', newspaper reviewers, and second-rate writers he dismisses. Most of us produce copy with the simple intention of communicating an opinion, a body of information, and a handful of ideas. If our writing has any impact, if it is at all remembered, it's because of what we say and not how we say it. Metcalf's essays, by contrast, shift the emphasis from the former to the latter. The concern with ideas is still there but the style has been foregrounded to such an extent that there are occasions when we pay less attention to the substance than to the style.

I can still scarcely credit that I've lived long enough to hear a professor of English criticizing a writer for writing elegantly and memorably. You seem to suggest, Sam, that to write well when most do not, and do not even attempt to, is to be somehow underhanded, unfair, *sneaky*. And it disheartens me a little, Sam, to hear you describe your own critical writing as 'copy'. But the real can of worms you uncork is your blithe acceptance of the idea that substance and style, form and content, are separable.

That damned 'something to say' again.

In an essay published in *The Second Macmillan Anthology*, Ray Smith wrote recently:

> The most important aesthetic perception a writer has is that the dichotomy between style and content is false, does not exist for a working artist. It should also be false for a reader reading or a critic cricketing; but you can't undo two millennia of western thought based upon the dichotomy.

To believe in such a dichotomy is to believe in the archetype of errors from which all errors flow. I am not going to argue this point. I am simply going to assert flatly that accepting the dichotomy is wrong. I *know* it is wrong. Every artist in the world knows it is wrong; our daily experience proves it.

To accept the dichotomy means that literature is seen as the 'vehicle' for ideas; it means that ideas must be considered literature's main purpose; it means that 'style' is seen as icing on the cake; it means that 'style', because seen as adventitious, can be ignored or belittled resulting in misreading and misunderstanding. To accept the dichotomy reduces literature to the pretty illustration of a thesis.

Pause, Sam, pause and think.

To accept this dichotomy leads away from art, leads downwards, inexorably downwards, delivers you up to barren theory and mindless intellectuality, abandons you at the last a broken figure in the sordid stews of Canadian criticism gripped by the fevered conviction that Rudy Wiebe is a major writer.

But in addition to embracing this reductive idea you also seem deeply *suspicious* of 'style' – if not antagonistic. In 'Some Kicks Against the Prick' you quote some remarks I'd made in an interview where I'd described D.H. Lawrence's work as 'clumsy, laborious, repetitive, and unsubtle' and Evelyn Waugh's as 'wonderful verbal performances of supreme elegance'. You go on to quote me as saying that I find Waugh's use of the semi-colon admirable and worthy of study. As indeed I do. Though you manage to make the very idea of the study of the use of the semi-colon sound an activity fit only for sniffers of lilies or the lower class of pederast.

And this provides another illumination of the temperamental differences between us. You with your 'something to say' and your uneasiness with style and me with my semi-colon claiming that the semi-colon *is* what is being said.

On one side of the balance, D.H. Lawrence; on the other, Evelyn Waugh.

Let's explore that suspicion and uneasiness a little further.

Of most of the story writers in this country whom I admire, you said in your essay that they 'could be said to represent an attitude to art similar to the one taken for granted by Flaubert's circle as well as, slightly later, by Mallarmé's'.

Some of those writers might wish to qualify that; Hugh Hood springs to mind.

You go on to quote Henry James's description of Flaubert's circle:

> What was discussed in that little smoke-clouded room was chiefly questions of taste, questions of art and form, and the speakers, for the most part, were, in aesthetic matter, radicals of the deepest dye. It would have been late in the day to propose among them any discussion of the relations of art to morality, any question as to the degree in which a novel might or might not concern itself with the teaching of a lesson.... The only duty of a novel was to be

well written; that merit included every other of which it was capable.

I infer from this that you feel that novels should be vehicles for 'morality' and that you come down on the side of novels 'teaching ... a lesson'. I also take it that you intend James's words as pretty basic and devastating criticism of a group of story writers who exhibit degenerate tendencies.

I, of course, accept any references to or comparisons with Flaubert as the hugest compliment.

Flaubert and Mallarmé. Pater and Wilde. From these writers flowed the theoretical thinking which underlies much of this century's literature. A brilliant consolidation and expression of that thinking was Wilde's essay 'The Decay of Lying', first published in 1889. The essay is in the form of a dialogue between two friends called Cyril and Vivian. Vivian is Wilde's mouthpiece; in what follows, he summarizes Wilde's aesthetic position:

Art never expresses anything but itself. It has an independent life, just as Thought has, and develops purely on its own lines....

The second doctrine is this. All bad art comes from returning to Life and Nature, and elevating them into ideals. Life and Nature may sometimes be used as part of Art's rough material, but before they are of any real service to art they must be translated into artistic conventions....

The third doctrine is that Life imitates Art far more than Art imitates Life....

It follows, as a corollary from this, that external Nature also imitates Art....

The final revelation is that Lying, the telling of beautiful untrue things, is the proper aim of Art.

Stagey, foppish, but at the same time brilliant and seminal, a word I have never managed to use before in a piece of writing.

Here, for absolutely no other reason than for its wit and sparkle, is Vivian persuading Cyril of the unlikely notion that external Nature copies Art:

Where, if not from the Impressionists, do we get those wonderful brown fogs that come creeping down our streets, blurring the gas-lamps and changing the houses into monstrous shadows? To whom, if not to them and their master, do we owe the lovely silver mists that brood over our river, and turn to faint forms of fading grace curved bridge and swaying barge? The extraordinary change that has taken place in the climate of London during the last ten years is entirely due to this particular school of Art. You smile. Consider the matter from a scientific or a metaphysical point of view, and you will find that I am right. For what is Nature? Nature is no great mother who has borne us. She is our creation. It is in our brain that she quickens to life. Things are because we see them, and what we see, and how we see it, depends on the Arts that have influenced us. To look at a thing is very different from seeing a thing. One does not see anything until one sees its beauty. Then, and then only, does it come into existence. At present, people see fogs, not because there are fogs, but because poets and painters have taught them the mysterious loveliness of such effects. There may have been fogs for centuries in London. I dare say there were. But no one saw them, and so we do not know anything about them. They did not exist till Art had invented them.

But let us stop enjoying ourselves and get back to the point.

The essence of what Wilde is saying here is that 'Art never expresses anything but itself.' This way of looking at and feeling about art is central to much of what has happened to art in this century. It emphasizes art's conventions, art's 'artiness'. It denies for art a didactic or moral purpose. It implies that the correct – indeed, the only possible – response to a painting or a book is a special kind of emotional response different in kind from other human emotions – an aesthetic response.

And here I must detour into a brief confession.

I do indeed believe that we need to respond to art in and on its own terms and I have taught such ideas consistently for twenty-five years. I do indeed believe that art has what Wilde calls 'an independent life' and that our task as readers is to put ourselves in touch with that life. Further, I've always believed and taught that the way to connect with that life is through an appreciation of the artificialities of technique and rhetoric. At the same time, however, I believe that the purpose of art is moral and that the effect of art is moral.

This would seem to be contradictory. Let us not beat about the bush. It *is* contradictory. This problem has troubled me since I was about eighteen. Aesthetic theory, however, is, I soon realized, a mug's game, the fastest way to a migraine known to man, the modern equivalent of angels on pin heads or guessing the number of beans in the bottle. My solution to the problem, arrived at after years of thought, was simply to stop thinking about it. I now say, at a brisk pace and hoping I won't be challenged, that although one's responses to art are aesthetic ones, these aesthetic responses convert themselves into emotional responses of a different kind, responses which connect us with the real world. I stress that this is a matter not untouched by mystery, a matter easier believed than explained – like, I spread my hands disarmingly – like, well, osmosis or transubstantiation. That sort of thing.

My inability to resolve contradictions remains *my* problem; it certainly isn't Oscar's. His theories and pronouncements are a strange mixture of languorous nonsense and cascading brilliance. He spoke often and vaguely of Beauty with a capital 'B' as being Art's end and purpose. Sometimes he seemed to suggest that Beauty was Art's morality. God only knows what he meant. But despite his posturings and provocations we are all intellectually and artistically in his debt.

Flaubert, Mallarmé, Pater, Whistler, Verlaine, Baudelaire –

these currents flowed through Wilde and 'the new aesthetics' flowed from him promulgating the subordination of all didactic purposes to what Wilde called 'the vital informing poetic principle' and celebrating the idea of art's 'independent life'. In some form or another, his ideas underpin much modern and contemporary practice.

Put very simply, Wilde steered us away from using art as a vehicle and towards the idea of art as an experience. He redefined the task of the audience; the audience no longer had to 'understand' the work – an external and intellectual activity – but rather had to enter into an emotional and aesthetic relationship with it on its terms.

Your disparagement, Sam, of the study of the use of semicolons and your scarcely veiled suggestion that such Flaubertian preoccupations are effete if not downright poofterish and your advocacy of the novel as a vehicle for 'ideas' and 'a world view' would seem to set you squarely against the trend of most writing in English in the twentieth century.

Temperament again.

The scope of stories is limited, you say, story writers are 'featherweights', 'the interesting action is elsewhere', stories are 'a minor form' – where shall I begin?

I'd remind you, Sam, that in the heavyweight division there was only ever *one* Muhammad Ali; the novel's lumbering norm is George Chuvalo. But I wouldn't for a moment attempt to downplay the novel's importance, though even as I'm saying this I realize that we are bound to value radically different *kinds* of novels.

I could not value as highly as you do Skvorecky's *The Engineer of Human Souls* – largely because it bulges with undigested chunks of 'something to say'. Nor can I share your enthusiasm for the novels of Rudy Wiebe – of whom more later. You, on the other hand, probably don't share my particular passion for Nathanael West's *Miss Lonelyhearts* and *The Day of the Locust* or Naipaul's *In a Free State* or Paul Scott's *Staying On.* In other words, if we imagine all writing as being on a continuum with poetry at one end, the novels I like will tend to be closer to poetry while those you like will tend to be up at the other end crowding philosophy and the essay. And I must confess, Sam, thinking of the whole tenor of your essay, of your seeming impatience with the particular and attraction towards idea and system, towards abstraction, that I wonder if it isn't philosophy or religion you're seeking.

You say in your essay that the novel can offer us 'a vision of human destiny' but that the short story 'usually gives local insights, visionary moments, epiphanies; instead of a world, a situation'.

I personally do not find the story form particularly limited in scope; it may not offer 'world views' but it certainly creates worlds and often creates them with a power and haunting intensity achieved by very few novels. Stories are not devoid of ideas – of course they're not – but they rarely present ideas overtly or didactically. That element of the story is not separable from the story's particularity and it emerges and suggests itself only after readers have experienced the story's world, only after we have shared in the story's performance. And that world and performance are made up of words and – I must say it – semi-colons set in motion.

Who could ever forget the worlds *these* stories create: 'The Daughters of the Late Colonel', 'Miss Brill', 'After the Storm', 'Hills like White Elephants', 'Araby', 'The Dead', 'The Snows of Kilimanjaro', 'Haircut', 'A Rose for Emily', 'A Good Man Is Hard to Find', 'Why I Live at the P.O.', 'A Visit of Charity', 'Livvie', 'The Chrysanthemums' – and here at home, 'A Small Piece of Blue', 'The Cocks Are Crowing', 'A North American Education', 'Flying a Red Kite', 'Getting to Williamstown', 'Irina', 'Royal Beatings', 'Dance of the Happy Shades'.

Are these 'featherweights'?

Is this 'minor' writing?

'The short story', you say,

... usually gives local insights, visionary moments, epiphanies; instead of a world, a situation. No wonder, then, that Metcalf wants to turn our attention to style and form; he is emphasizing the story's one undoubted strength: its scope may be limited but its world is perfectly organized. No wonder, also, that if we apply Metcalf's distorting view of fiction to the novel, Evelyn Waugh, that brilliant writer but second-rank novelist, is preferred to a giant like Lawrence.

There again is that acceptance of the dichotomy between form and content, the demand for intellectualization, the refusal or inability to connect with the story's particularity, with its 'vital informing poetic principle'. But because we occupy positions on opposite sides of a great temperamental divide, we could argue in abstract terms into the small hours. Instead, let us examine my 'distorting view of fiction'. If you consider Eudora Welty and Alice Munro and Flannery O'Connor as 'featherweights' and their writing as 'minor', let's look at the writing of D.H. Lawrence, a writer you describe as 'a giant'.

When I was about eighteen, I discovered one of the loveliest books about writing ever written – *Enemies of Promise* by Cyril Connolly. It had a profound effect on me, focusing my unfledged attention on language, rhythm, texture, rhetoric, and tone – a focus Sam would doubtless deplore. And focusing it in a way that made the related efforts of my tutor, L.C. Knights, seem spinsterish. It was all a marvellous antidote to the lumpy and inedible defector and Eastern Bloc fiction which appeared at that time in nearly every issue of *Encounter* – fiction I expect Sam would rather approve of. Even at eighteen, I thought I'd scream if I had to read one more story by Abram Tertz.

A couple of paragraphs in *Enemies of Promise* suggested to me a way of reading to which I gave, and still give, complete assent:

So much depends on style, this factor of which we are growing more and more suspicious, that although the tendency of criticism is to explain a writer either in terms of his sexual experience or his economic background, I still believe his technique remains the soundest base for a diagnosis, that it should be possible to learn as much about an author's income and sex-life from one paragraph of his writing as from his cheque stubs and his love-letters, and that one should also be able to learn how well he writes, and who are his influences. Critics who ignore style are liable to lump good and bad writers together in support of preconceived theories.

An expert should be able to tell a carpet by one skein of it; a vintage by rinsing a glassful round his mouth. Applied to prose there is one advantage attached to this method – a passage taken from its context is isolated from the rest of a book, and cannot depend on the goodwill which the author has cleverly established with his reader.

You mention with special approval in 'Some Kicks Against the Prick' Lawrence's *The Rainbow*. Here is a passage from the opening chapter describing the routine of life on the Brangwen farm. Let's rinse a glassful of this vintage round our mouths:

But heaven and earth was teeming around them, and how should this cease? They felt the rush of the sap in spring, they knew the wave which cannot halt, but every year throws forward the seed to begetting, and, falling back, leaves the young-born on the earth. They knew the intercourse between heaven and earth, sunshine drawn into the breast and bowels, the rain sucked up in the daytime, nakedness that comes under the wind in autumn, showing the birds' nests no longer worth hiding. Their life and interrelations were such; feeling the pulse and body of the soil, that opened to their furrow for the grain, and became smooth and supple after their ploughing, and clung to their feet with a weight that pulled like desire, lying hard and unresponsive when the crops were to be shorn away. The young corn waved and was silken, and the lustre slid along the limbs of the men who saw it. They took the udder of the cows, the cows yielded milk and pulse against the hands of the men, the pulse of the blood of the teats of the cows beat into the pulse of the hands of the men. They mounted their horses, and held life between the grip of their knees, they harnessed their horses at the wagon, and, with hand on the bridle-rings, drew the heaving of the horses after their will.

This is extraordinary writing. But what exactly is it all about? What is being described? Obviously, Lawrence is not attempting to describe realistically the daily round of chores. Though he can write with loving detail when he wishes, there is nothing here of the realities of byre and midden.

What do the sentences and phrases *mean*?

'... sunshine drawn into the breast and bowels ...'

'... feeling the pulse and body of the soil ...'

'The young corn waved and was silken, and the lustre slid along the limbs of the men who saw it.'

How do you respond to this, Sam? Doesn't the fact that it's gibberish bother you? Are you able to ignore such questions in your enthusiasm for Lawrence's 'world view'? *How can you believe that Lawrence's 'world view' exists independently of the words and sentences in which it is couched?*

The rhythms of the paragraph derive at a rather phoney remove from those of the Bible and the intention is not description but incantation. Nothing wrong with that except that the spell's ill-made. There is something lugubriously funny about the language describing the blood relationship between milkers and cows and, about the passage as a whole, a self-consciousness, a straining after elevation, a faint hysteria. Why is it all so easy to parody? Why am I so instantly reminded of Stella Gibbons' *Cold Comfort Farm* where characters are always muttering darkly and obscurely of the sexual forces which will be unleashed in the coming spring when the sukebind be in flower?

Here for those sensible souls who cherish parody is the primeval Reuben from *Cold Comfort Farm* gazing for the first time upon his cousin Flora Poste:

> His thoughts swirled like a beck in spate behind the sodden grey furrows of his face. A woman ... Blast! Blast! Come to wrest away from him the land whose love fermented in his veins, like slow yeast. She-woman. Young, soft-coloured, insolent. His gaze was suddenly edged by a fleshy taint. Break her. Break. Keep and hold and hold fast the land. The land, the iron furrows of frosted earth under the rain-lust, the fecund spears of rain, the swelling, slow burst of seed-sheaths, the slow smell of cows and cry of cows, the trampling bride-path of the bull in his hour. All his, his ...

Not *wildly* more preposterous than Lawrence, is it?

My grandfather was a coal miner in the British midlands living in a jerry-built company-owned house with a stand pipe in the communal yard for water, so I know something firsthand of the world Lawrence described. I also know its farms and countryside. Lawrence's vaunted sensuality and rather self-conscious paganism were a reaction to that particular British background of industrial spoliation and sour, puritan nonconformity. His poems and travel writing and novellas – indeed, his very life – spoke to me when I was young of larger possibilities. So now when I find it difficult to read much of his writing for sheer embarrassment, I'm not going to go out of my way to belabour his obvious defects.

He remains a prophet whom time and massive social change have left stranded. While I wasn't looking, time has turned him into an historical figure. Surely there cannot be many people under fifty whose sex-life approximates the norm who read him now with the same excitement I once read him? Perhaps, like Keats, he has become a writer best tasted when one is young.

Evelyn Waugh, on the other hand, whom you describe as 'brilliant writer but second-rank novelist' – a distinction I think

I'd be incapable of making, or even understanding – is as contemporary now as then. The *Sword of Honour* trilogy grows in stature while *Decline and Fall*, published in 1928, still has the dew of its creation on it.

But if for sentimental reasons I'm reluctant to comment further on Lawrence, I'm not reluctant to consider other writing that you, Sam, describe as 'great'; doing so should cast more light on the temperamental differences governing our approaches to literature. If you are going to dismiss or disparage an entire genre as 'minor' writing, then it is important that readers should see examples of what you would consider major writing for you are, after all, one of the critical élite whose judgements mould literary opinion.

Let me re-quote from 'Some Kicks Against the Prick':

Not unexpectedly, the only time that we see major claims being made for writers like Mansfield or Welty and the inevitable handful of others is in essays like Metcalf's where a *parti pris* critic or writer is asserting the importance of the sub-genre. Everyone else takes it for granted that a great writer can throw off a story between chapters of a novel. Obviously I exaggerate, but I can't help thinking of Tolstoy, James, Lawrence, Faulkner, and Hemingway, who move easily between the two forms. Rudy Wiebe – Metcalf's most obvious blind spot – Hugh Hood, and Jack Hodgins are the Canadian examples that come to mind.

But before rinsing round our mouths a glassful of my 'most obvious blind spot', Rudy Wiebe, I would point out that Wiebe has not 'thrown off' many stories at all whether between chapters or otherwise and those which he *has* thrown off, with the exception of 'Where Is the Voice Coming From?', are not wildly distinguished.

My first example – chosen more or less at random – is from Wiebe's novel *My Lovely Enemy*:

'You believe in a god as people always have, to quote you, a god to whom you pray about future events in hope that he'll manipulate them in some way and benefit you – your god can change the future?'

'If he pleases, of course, well?'

When I was a businessman we had met just as often, which is annually at Albert and Ardyth's spring party, and she had never bothered to snipe at what she supposed I believed, but now – perhaps my present label sets her off: I am a 'professor', to 'profess' is very different than to 'business', ah, to leave a name at which the world grows pale.

'Well, if your god has the power to change the future, at your request, then surely at your request he can also change the past.'

'Of course', I said, much too quickly.

'But that,' Joy had at me squarely with her main thrust, 'that is patently ridiculous and if you're an historian you know it.'

'What do you mean, *if* I'm an historian?'

'Well, you are, so you know it's ridiculous. You dig around in the past as if – you know you do – as if it had already all happened, whatever you find is absolutely unchangeable. Could you,' she was very nearly laughing now: only a defeated opponent could make her name come true, 'the most famous event in your area, could you pray that Louis Riel should not be hanged, today, right now in 1980? And your god would answer your prayer – suddenly Riel would *not* have been hanged?'

But she did not quite laugh; her eyes below her plucked brows suddenly gained a clear grey wideness; almost like distant longing. Perhaps I just wanted to see that, groping frantically as I was to distract her historical absurdity; I tried peevishness.

'Oh it's always that praying Riel, don't you know of anyone else in the nineteenth century, always –'

'What does it matter who?'

'Try Darcy McGee, George A. Custer, anyone.'

'I don't know McGee [I nearly roared!] and Custer was involved with Indians, I wouldn't want to make it too complicated for your Christian god.'

'So considerate!'

'Well? He's not hanged?' Her philosophic bloodhounds undetracted.

'You choose Riel, I suppose, because his death is a very commonly known [she did not notice my McGee jab] "hard historic fact", as it were?'

She hesitated; I might out-expert her. 'He was hanged in 1885, wasn't he?'

I said *is*, not *was*, it is right now a hard historic fact, you'd say?'

'Yes, okay, yes, *is*.'

'In other words, the actual action of the hanging is completed, now. Riel is not being hanged now, in Regina or anywhere else.'

'Yes of course. So?'

I wasn't sure of 'so' myself, but I had to keep throwing out the, in this case, rotten fish of Professor Becker's argument since at the moment my flailing mind striated by wine could seem to hook into nothing else.

'You're talking', I continued, 'not about changing the actual historical event but about changing the record of that event [I was contradicting my own operational theory and attempted practice, but she could not know that], which is a very different thing. Because historians always deal exclusively with the records, not with the events themselves which happen only once and are, by the very nature of human life, unrepeatable. History after all is not physics. The historian must reach conclusions using all the miscellaneous and often chance records of all sorts of people who observed with untrained eyes something which certainly wasn't as controlled as even the sloppiest laboratory experiment, and their observations can never be tested for accuracy by any repetition.

What can be said about the writing of this scene? The most obvious observation first: Wiebe has very little dramatic sense. The conversation is not *built*. Any possible rising tension is constantly interrupted and diluted by commentary. It is, to put it charitably, *uncommon* to find a fictional character who comments on his own dialogue as he is speaking it. Wiebe's intrusive square brackets are preposterous.

A second observation: can one *hear* this conversation? Do we believe in these voices speaking to us? Do we believe the syntax? Do we believe the rhythms? Is there any sense of a party, of other people, of noise, of other conversations surrounding the conversation we're supposed to be hearing? Did this conversation ever take place? Or is it the cardboard stuff of a pre-existing argument chopped up into lengths?

A third observation: on the evidence of this extract, we might begin to suspect that Wiebe has a tin ear.

I wonder what Cyril Connolly would have deduced from *this* sentence: 'I wasn't sure of "so" myself, but I had to keep throwing out the, in this case, rotten fish of Professor Becker's argument since at the moment my flailing mind striated by wine could seem to hook into nothing else.'

The mixture of metaphor in 'flailing' and 'hook' is enough to make one wince but the word 'striated' coming between them adds to the rich confusion. The writing gives an overall impression of stumbling clumsiness.

Any writer who is described as 'major' should surely be in command of the basic techniques of his craft. Wiebe patently isn't. He couldn't play a scale. Credible and persuasive dialogue is always an invention, always highly artificial. It is first a matter of *hearing* and then secondly, a matter of formalizing and inventing how one has heard. If you want to read dialogue credibly performed, try, oh, Elmore Leonard, say, or Loren D. Estleman.

This sort of thing, from Elmore Leonard's novel *City Primeval*:

> Hunter was saying to the young black guy, 'How well did you know Adele Simpson?'
>
> 'I never seen her before right then.'
>
> 'You took her purse – what else?'
>
> 'What purse you talking about?'
>
> 'Darrold, you had Adele Simpson's credit cards on you.'
>
> 'I found 'em.'
>
> Hunter said, 'You gonna start shucking me again, Darrold? We're talking about murder, man, not a little half-assed assault. You understand me, mandatory life ...'
>
> Raymond got up from his desk. He walked over to the young black guy in the plaid golf hat and touched him on the shoulder.
>
> 'Let me ask you something, okay?'
>
> The young black guy didn't answer, but looked up at the lieutenant.
>
> 'The woman's lying there dead – is that right?'
>
> 'What I been trying to tell him.'
>
> 'What did you burn her with?'
>
> The young black guy didn't answer.
>
> 'Shit,' Hunter said, 'let's put him upstairs.'
>
> 'I just touch her a little,' the young black guy said then, 'see if she's alive.'
>
> Hunter said, 'What'd you touch her with, your dick?'
>
> 'No man, nothing like that.'
>
> 'They're doing an autopsy on her', Hunter said. 'Now they find any semen in her and it matches your blood type – then we got to ask you, Darrold, you rape her before or after you shot her?'
>
> 'I *didn't* shoot her. You find a gun on me? Shit no.'
>
> 'Where'd you touch her?' Raymond asked.

After a moment the young black guy said, 'Like around her legs.'

'Just touched her a little?'

'Yeah, just, you know, a little bit.'

'You touch her with a cigarette?' Raymond asked.

'Yeah, I believe was a cigarette.'

'Lit cigarette?'

'Yeah, was smoked down though, you know, like a butt.'

'Why'd you touch her with a cigarette?'

'I told you,' the young black guy said, 'see if she's alive, tha's all.'

Any writer might envy the subtlety of such dialogue; the last few lines, in particular, move with great restraint and delicacy.

I'm making no major claims for Elmore Leonard. In addition to thrillers, he writes Westerns. He is an entertainer and a writer of genre fiction. But to dismiss his work as 'dime store fiction' would be very foolish indeed. He is a vastly talented craftsman whose dialogue could teach an aspiring young writer more than years spent in Creative Writing classes. And he's far from being alone on those revolving wire racks.

The sad truth is that you can buy better writing than Rudy Wiebe's seven days a week at any Mac's Milk.

In the 'Introduction' to the New Canadian Library edition of Wiebe's *The Blue Mountains of China*, Professor W.J. Keith wrote:

When the history of fiction in the twentieth century comes to be written, one of the main criticisms to be levelled against our contemporary novelists may well be that they bring an impressive array of technical sophistication and expertise to bear upon subject-matter that, far too often, is trivial or unworthy. If so, Rudy Wiebe will certainly be remembered as an honourable exception. Not that he is unconcerned about technique; on the contrary, the

exquisite artistry of *The Blue Mountains of China* is what
ensures it a place among the finest novels written in Canada – or anywhere else, for that matter – in our time.

Later in the 'Introduction' W.J. Keith writes:

... here was a novelist with a breadth of vision, seriousness
of purpose and (above all) a dazzling artistry that I had met
with elsewhere only in novelists whose names are household words wherever great literature is read.

To be fair, W.J. Keith *does* speak of 'the tendency towards the
ponderous, the rather angular stolidity that lends an impression
of stiffness' to Wiebe's writing, and of 'certain syntactical
awkwardnesses in Wiebe's style', but these reservations apply
only to Wiebe's earliest work. *The Blue Mountains of China*, W.J.
Keith concludes, is marked by 'seemingly effortless artistry'.

When I first read this effusion written by a critic I respect, I
considered giving up literature in favour of something more
intellectually rigorous – like tiddly-winks.

Let's have a look at this 'dazzling artistry'. In the following
extract two ladies are discussing Stephen Vizinczey's *In Praise of
Older Women* and Leonard Cohen's *Beautiful Losers*:

'This certainly wasn't around when I was here at Christmas', she tossed the book in Rachel's lap. 'Placed for my
consolation?'

'Heavens!' Rachel was sitting on the bed, laughing, 'I'm
almost embarrassed!'

'Why aren't you completely? It doesn't at all look like
something left by the Gideons. If you keep up such
thoughtfulness next time in Toronto I'll have to retreat to a
hotel.'

'I read it here because I didn't want Alex to see me',
Rachel's face was slightly red but her eyes still laughed.

They had known each other too intimately for too many years to be embarrassed for themselves.

'Has it? Well, I'm the usual professor's wife, about two years behind. Lydia Fern says it's the latest thing for us "older women" to read.'

Elizabeth picked up the book and looked again at the woman on the cover. 'Did you like it?'

'Me? It's just to read so you can look around brightly, in all your worldly wisdom. Half the first half I can't believe and three-quarters of the last is repetition.'

'Quintessenally [sic] quartered. Who are all these older women he praises, how old are they?'

'That's the trouble! They're mostly about thirty, or thirty-five.'

They laughed together, seeing themselves; women well enough taken care of but too close to fifty to expect a passing male's notice, unless they smiled hard.

'It has at least wit?' Elizabeth said, folding her blouses carefully.

'Yes,' Rachel hesitated on the word, 'but not really. There is one rather funny spot, I think. He's – the over-powering-animal hero – rolling in the grass with this semi-reluctant wife who can't quite make up her mind – or whatever she has to make up – and at the great moment the husband comes snorting along in the dark and he has to finish business more or less in his pocket.'

'Wit?'

'Well – wittier than soap opera. But with the children on their own and Alex finally at that text, so tied up with committees too, and there isn't that much to do in the house –' Rachel stopped, suddenly sober. 'Liesel, do you have enough, living by yourself?'

'Do I – get enough?'

'Oh you!'

The familiar childish name had caught at Elizabeth in

annoyance. They had been such honest friends for so long because they never asked about intimacies unless the other began by offering her own, and at that moment it seemed to her Rachel had overstepped in their laughter; she continued, tone bright and sharp, 'I had quite enough of marriage five years with José, thank you.' Rachel was looking away; 'Sorry', Elizabeth said. 'I guess that reveals something; even after twenty-two years I unearth that rat.'

'Everybody makes mistakes when they're young.'

'Of course. And some just learn for life. Well, if you like dirty books that are witty, so-called, have you seen *Beautiful Losers?*'

'I've seen it – in the University Library and it looked like such a lovely title I picked it up. Heavens!'

'If you can stomach it, it does have wit, of a kind. But literally rather more – to avoid the obvious Anglo-Saxon – excreta. Some "great" Canadian critics say it's "the great" Canadian novel at last.'

'Really? Somehow I couldn't get started.'

'There is a martyred Iroquois – Huron? – princess in it who mutilates herself with thorns, which is rather unoriginal but –'

'Perhaps she rides them', Rachel suggested with interest.

'That's good, I wonder if Lennie – but that's not too clear, along with everything else. Lucidity today is strictly for morons. And the girl is truly most pure but there are these lecherous old men who – ahh – shall we say are "adlingulating" her toes, one by one –'

'Ad—what?'

'Adlingulate? I just made it up. English needs such a word; like "osculate" for "kiss" – sounds much more proper for us older, rather oldest, women. Come now, remember your Latin: "lingua"?'

'The tongue?'

'One hundred percent. There are all these old men –'

'The priests?'

'Correct again! Rachel, you really –'

'And there must be a sexy Jew. Maybe homosexual or at least ambivalent, but fighting his Jewishness, or better, a WASP dreaming he's a Jew and – yes, that's it – a WASP as Jew burning himself on the martyr fire of the princess, you know, a faggot for the fire still "adlingulating" her metatarsal extremities as he transpires to symbolize repentance for all the horrid things Christian bigots have –'

'Good heavens, Rachel! And "transpires"!'

'Use your Latin! Wonderful! It's The Great Canadian Novel at last! Hasn't it got an Eskimo? A Presbyterian and a dirty RCMP?'

'No. That part is in 1680, there weren't RCMP or Jews in Can—'

'It doesn't matter, a Presbyterian is enough. It's still the great Canadian novel even with just the priests and the Indian toes. It's got everything: race, sex, Freud, religion, and inhibited Canadians: the frustrated priests working off their childish oral-oriented perversions on the pure-beautiful-twinkling-sexy toes of the sexless Indian maiden. Whoopee! I have to read it.'

'Oh don't, Rachel. The book will simply confuse all your brilliant clarity! Alex must find a place for you at York; I must write him as soon as I get home; you must give a lecture on –'

'Liesel!'

'– to avoid all Anglo-Saxon again – on The Intercourse, Excreta and Adlingulating School in Canadian literature. Fantastic! Our own literary Group of Seventeen or "Layteen".'

'You absolute witch!'

'The Princess Tekakwitha is not sexless. That exactly she is not.'

'You've ruined my great Canadian novel', Rachel sat up where she had collapsed on the bed. 'Keep your half-hearted recommendations to yourself; you won't let me have my moment of brilliance; just when you compliment you wreck it all by topping me.'

'Watch that very complex word "top". It's Anglo-Saxon too!'

They literally tumbled together with laughter. Finally they sat up, and Elizabeth said, 'See here, you crushed all these blouses, contorting yourself in so un-matronly a manner. That is a fact, like the fact of the pulchritudinous princess. And I did not wreck your startling insight into the Canadian male, old men who've leaked away their zip....'

Again, what can one say? This is another conversation that never took place. By now, we have proof positive that Wiebe has a tin ear. There is a simpering and tee-hee quality about the dialogue which suggests Benny Hill and Frankie Howerd in drag. Surely I don't have to demonstrate, line by awful line, the absolute impossibility of this stuff as speech?

Surely no one other than Bill Keith and Sam Solecki is dazzled by this sample of Wiebe's 'effortless artistry'? I'm beginning to feel with Louis Armstrong who is supposed to have answered a lady's question about what jazz *was* by saying: 'Lady, if you've gotta ask, you ain't never going to know.'

The writing is ponderous and inept; it reminds me of a circus elephant mounting its tub and heaving its vast sad bulk into a begging position.

If this verbiage strikes W.J. Keith as 'dazzling artistry', he ought to have his ears examined.

Wiebe's tin ear plagues him even when he isn't writing dialogue. Here is a final example from *My Lovely Enemy*. The prose is dense, clotted, awkward. It is difficult to read aloud. Its rhythms do not shape and form its meanings. It contorts itself into crippled shapes and lurches. It is prose which is – in the root sense of the word – *barbarous*:

'You have a foreskin.'

'Midwives on prairie farms don't carry knives', I tell the high ceiling.

She senses my self-deprecation; bitterness perhaps. 'A foreskin is lovely', touching it. 'It's barbaric to cut it off.'

'Necessary sanitary, they say.'

'Barbarism, Jewish barbarism.'

'Every day, remember my bush beginnings.'

'Every day?'

'Sanitary you know, above all.'

'It makes you nice and pointed.'

Fingers reading me, a coming to my senses like sunlight searching in folds, along edges and strangely the small worm of my daily life curls warmer and without a dream of volition, only limpness. Unpredictably stupid body, unfathomable when it should be obvious, I certainly cannot look at her curved sideways to me, certainly breathing up now to find my eye. Is this overwhelming ... romance or an annual conversation with myself in my doctor's office, no, I don't have to get up at night, no, I'm monotonously regular, yes, a glass of juice every morning, now the pads of her fingers are round and smooth ... my head tilts to her face classical as Nefertiti, black eyes now unwinking and dilated in the brilliant light. Her eyelashes flicker to my sudden small surge.

There is another conversation we are not having. I see words run across her inconceivable cheekbones, a finger writing   the morning sunlight   where have you been never anywhere before   are you alone   yes will you dare see me in daylight   will you let me try   whom did you bring with you   no one either   really   yes if words were wrens they would be written on the air   like spider roads yes   blazing threads of sunlight.

Her hand leaves, in silence. 'Excuse me', with a sudden long movement she is over me and walking across light to the bathroom. I will not think. Poster wisdom has it love is never having to say you're sorry, the CPR should plaster that on ceilings, presumably the beloved enjoys crushing, desires needles through the gut, presumably no lover would inflict that, imbecilic presumption, who the more easily can? Love is not love that alters when it alteration finds, o no it is an ever-fixed mark, o no it is a flat-footed morning bathroom necessity, o yes it is a short-sighted blur sprayed about by radiance, a shining between legs while a toilet rushes somewhere scissoring closer, separate as devastating nightmares. 'All lovers live by longing, and endure: / Summon a vision and declare it pure.' She lifts back sheet and blanket and forks herself astride naked me, kneeling wide-kneed with her strong thighs faintly fuzzed, blondish there not black, the look down her long nose steadily deliberate. Lips open.

Wiebe displays here an astonishing array of inelegancies and misjudgements. It is advisable for writers to avoid perpetrating scenes of torrid congress; the description of human sexual activity tends – usually unintentionally – towards the risible.

Writing about sexual intercourse also leads, inevitably, to other vices. Such as euphemism. And strained comparisons.

It is *always* advisable to avoid mention or depiction of the male member for there is something hopelessly and inherently comic about the damn thing. Like Punch, it's always popping up to undermine order and decorum. It's a rare writer who can break this rule.

Knobs and Nefertiti, you might say, don't mix.

(It will doubtless be claimed that Wiebe has thematic reasons for describing his protagonist's member as a Blakean 'worm' but a worm is a worm and a member is a member and the metaphor, however thematically and intellectually appropriate, remains ludicrous.)

Far too many prose writers when they want to crank up the emotional decibels descend to the bathos of pseudo-poetry. Some of them even *quote* poetry. Instead of honing their prose even finer and cutting in right to the bone of the observable world, they wallow in lush language and smear their lenses with Vaseline as if they were filming dreamy TV ads for Tampax.

There is little more embarrassing than faked lyricism.

'... yes if words were wrens they would be written on the air ...'

Yes, and if my aunt had balls she'd be my uncle.

Faked lyricism usually verges on the incomprehensible because it is in retreat from particularity; because it isn't *looking* at the world, it usually gets its facts wrong. Wiebe's spasm here concerning wrens is presumably meant to evoke something like birds warbling joyously on high in a sky of blue. Or something. Your guess is as good as mine. *Warblers*, perhaps. Larks. That sort of thing. The problem with wrens is that they are shy birds whose habitat is tangled undergrowth and deep woods. In the West, they typically inhabit canyons. They tend to flit from shadow to shade and rarely fly more than a couple of feet above the ground.

I do assure you that I am being more than picky.

Someone – it may actually have been Sam Solecki – described Wiebe as an 'experimental' writer. There are departures from the orthodox in this present sample but it is misleading to present Wiebe as one who is extending the boundaries of conventional writing. The visual devices Wiebe uses here to suggest unspoken thoughts – spaces instead of periods and a lack of capital letters at the beginnings of sentences – do not translate effectively. The mind has to grope through the sets of words to make sure that they are assembled in meaningful phrases or sentences; in effect, the mind has to insert periods. Wiebe fails, therefore, in suggesting the speed and lightness of unspoken conversation. Instead of language dancing, he has delivered a laborious construct.

Wiebe writes for the eye.

There is rarely for me in Wiebe's writing surprise and delight in language and device. His language rarely forces me to see anew. His language rarely *ambushes* me. Over every scene is the earnest pall of his 'something to say' couched in language which is plodding and discordant.

If I had to find one adjective to sum up Wiebe's writing, I think that word would be 'gauche'.

My interest in all this is not to assault Wiebe's reputation but rather to illuminate the thinking and feeling that lie behind the judgement of two of our foremost critics. I do not for a moment doubt Wiebe's intellectual abilities. Nor do I doubt the depth and strength of his religious and moral convictions. I am simply saying that he has failed in transmuting these convictions into art.

Sam Solecki and Bill Keith have made large – if not extraordinary – claims for Wiebe's writing. They are both influential teachers at one of our most important universities. They are both arbiters of taste. Their evaluative accounts of modern fiction in *The Oxford Companion to Canadian Literature* are literary history in the making. My question to both of them is simple: how can one be a duly accredited *arbiter elegantiae* and endorse so ringingly writing which is so obviously inept?

We seem to be facing a peculiar question: can a badly-written book be an important book? By 'important' I don't mean important in a journalistic, sociological, or historical sense. *Uncle Tom's Cabin,* for example, was an important crusading book when it was written and is important now for historical reasons, but I'm asking the question of contemporary *literary* work. Can a contemporary literary work be both ill-written and important as literature? It's obvious from everything I've said that I would dismiss such a question as simply silly but – on the evidence – Sam and Bill might not.

If Sam can dismiss an entire genre of immense sophistication as 'featherweight' in favour of such stuff as Rudy Wiebe's indigestible duff and if Bill considers duff the stuff of 'dazzling artistry' ...

I'VE BEEN TRYING throughout this essay to show that Sam and I – and, by extension, critics and writers – look at writing in very different ways. I have suggested that there are fundamental differences between us which are less intellectual at base than temperamental.

It would probably be fair to say that most critics are concerned with *what* is being said which is an element they are always trying to extract from a work and which they quite obviously believe somehow exists outside the actual words, phrases, and semi-colons in which this 'what' is couched. Most writers regard this belief on the part of critics as evidence of mental retardation.

I'd like to end, Sam, by making a plea to you and to Bill and to other critics to pay much greater attention to the idea of putting yourselves in touch with a work's 'vital informing principle' by giving yourselves up to the process of the story, to its performance. I am, in brief, urging on you a different *kind* of knowing, a different *kind* of understanding. Your present approach to the story might be compared to that of the person who stands in front of an abstract painting demanding to know what it 'means'; the asking of that question precludes any kind of answer. To give yourself up to the story's performance means that as a participant in the story's rhetoric you can no longer simply ignore or overlook rhetoric which is inept in your quest for 'what the story is saying' because you will have renounced any such quest before entering the story.

We – and here I'll make bold to speak for other writers – we would all agree with Waugh's comments in 'Literary Style in England and America' that 'style is not a seductive decoration added to a functional structure' but is rather 'the essence of a work of art'. We would all, I think, give assent to Waugh's statement quoted as an epigraph to this essay that it is only the recluse at the desk, a writer concerned 'more and more with Style', who stands any chance at all of 'giving abiding pleasure to others'.

We all feel deeply and passionately about semi-colons, about pauses and silences, about sounds and rhythms and weights. We are passionate about these technicalities of rhetoric for a very good reason; we are passionate about them because we have always known that *our* 'something to say' lives in and through them and is inseparable from them. The words of our stories are the worlds of our stories.

In a piece that Alice Munro wrote for an anthology of mine entitled *Making It New*, she describes how she reads stories by other people and how she wants hers read. She implicitly rejects Sam's 'something to say' – she calls that a road taking her to a destination – and appeals instead for an *experiencing* of the story's world.

We are both saying the same sort of thing in different ways:

I will start by explaining how I read stories written by other people. For one thing, I can start reading them anywhere; from beginning to end, from end to beginning, from any point in between in either direction. So obviously I don't take up a story and follow it as if it were a road, taking me somewhere, with views and neat diversions along the way. I go into it, and move back and forth and settle here and there, and stay in it for a while. It's more like a house. Everybody knows what a house does, how it encloses space and makes connections between one enclosed space and another and presents what is outside in a new way. This is the nearest I can come to explaining what a story does for me, and what I want my stories to do for other people.

Stories, I repeat, are to be experienced. And it is through language, rhythm, texture, rhetoric, and tone that we experience them.

A Dream of Laocoön

Prologue

SATURDAY, 12 NOVEMBER 1988 (John Metcalf's fiftieth birthday): I'm sitting in a conference room at the College Motor Inn on the outskirts of Guelph listening to John as he delivers the 'world première' (as musicians would say) of his latest critical diatribe, 'Dear Sam'. Half-way through, as he had warned in some introductory remarks, it suddenly turns into 'Dear Bill' as he ridicules my conviction that Rudy Wiebe is a writer of considerable stature. Sam Solecki has been unable to attend, so I jot down a few notes as various objections and arguments occur to me. When he finishes, I anticipate a lively, perhaps heated discussion. But, like a hairy benevolent gnome, Tim Struthers jumps up and hastily brings the conference to a close. 'You mean I don't get any chance to reply?' I ask. There are smiles, but adjournment has been announced. The group breaks up.

TWO WEEKS LATER: A phone-call from Struthers. Plans are afoot. There is a general feeling that the debate should continue. I had more to say, hadn't I? (Well, yes.) How about a reprinting of Sam's original article, updated, followed by 'Dear Sam', followed by a commentary from me? (Well, why not?) A tentative schedule is arranged.

THURSDAY, 15 DECEMBER: Submerged in essay-marking and an assortment of academic chores. These last include adding some minor revisions to a book-length manuscript on Canadian fiction entitled – will you believe it? – *A Sense of Style*. At lunchtime the Christmas mail brings, along with begging-letters from dubious charities and seasonal greetings that display a bothersome range of artistic taste, a typescript of 'Dear Sam'. Plus a letter in John's elegant and inimitable handwriting:

> I shall read your article in reply to 'Dear Sam' with wonder
> and with the scrutiny I'd give to Houdini – because as far as
> I can see you're chained, padlocked, locked in a chest, and
> under water.

I read the typescript of 'Dear Sam' – forty-five pages of it – with continuing reservations about the argument but unqualified admiration for the style. Style, the crucial factor in this whole exchange. Gloom. I'm expected to enter the fray with one of the finest (and rapier-adept) stylists in the country. Why do I get myself into these messes? Houdini's chains clank. And clank.

FRIDAY, 16 DECEMBER: I wake in the early hours of the morning, from troubled but unremembered dreams, thinking about Laocoön, and a statue I've never seen. *Laocoön?* Then a visual image of encircling snakes like Houdini's chains. (Even as I doze I register, with gratitude and amusement, that the image comes 'courtesy of John Metcalf'.) What does it mean? Can the statue of Laocoön represent my equivalent to John's Ling Feng-Mien watercolour? The unconscious moves, to be sure, in wondrous ways. Metaphoric lights flash, and in an instant I begin to see how Laocoön will figure in this curious snagged controversy. But not yet. The image will return when needed. Meanwhile, let's begin.

1. On the Propagation of Masterpieces

DEAR JOHN: There is, of course, one overwhelming reason why I'm delighted to take part in this three-cornered argument. Sam and yourself, for all your disagreements, have at least one quality in common: you are both courageous enough to raise highly controversial issues which most modern literary commentators (especially academics) prefer to side-step. Moreover, these are the issues that matter. The *real* issues. No high-flown talk about signifiers, narratology, and the diachronic; no fashionable twaddle about the death of the author and the ambiguous pleasures of pure textuality. Instead, hard-hitting arguments in clear and vivid language about how we read and what we ought to read. Back (as you might say) to basics.

Or – dare I make the point in more provocatively mischievous terms? – both of you have 'something to say'.

So far as I am concerned, John, you've focused the argument, brilliantly, in your anecdote about the Piazza della Signoria, Michelangelo's *David,* and the Japanese tourist, followed by the parallel trio of Assisi, the Giotto and Cimabue frescoes, and Ling Feng-Mien's *Java Sparrows on a Wisteria Bough.* It's a splendid parable – by which I mean once again, I'm afraid, that it has 'something to say'. But you've presented the issue in the right way, in personal and human terms: how do we respond – ultimately, honestly – to high art?

I'm reminded of an earlier dear Sam, Samuel Butler in *The Way of All Flesh,* commenting on Mendelssohn's self-congratulatory two hours as he admires the classic sculpture and painting in the Tribune:

> I wonder how many chalks Mendelssohn gave himself for having sat two hours on that chair. I wonder how often he looked at his watch to see if his two hours were up.... But perhaps if the truth were known his two hours was not quite two hours.

Or Henry James's Christopher Newman, in *The American,* 'reclining at his ease on the great circular divan which at that period occupied the centre of the Salon Carré, in the Museum of the Louvre', gazing not at the paintings but at 'those innumerable young women in irreproachable toilets who devote themselves, in France, to the propagation of masterpieces', and, after suffering 'an aesthetic headache' from too much culture, admitting that 'he had often admired the copy much more than the original'. Or (closer to home) in Jack Hodgins' *The Honorary Patron*, a young man stomping out of the Art Gallery of Ontario collection of Henry Moore's reclining figures and uttering the ambivalent comment: 'They make me feel stupid!'

A human being, a work of art, and honesty. It's an unpredictable combination.

I read your parable, John, with delight; and I share, totally, your mixed feelings. But when I read your exegesis – along with those parts of Sam's commentary to which you object – I find myself disagreeing with both of you in apparently small but actually significant details. I part company with Sam when he argues: 'In the sense of the phrase intended by Pasternak, most short story writers have nothing to say, and we don't expect it of them any more than we expect an epic poem from a lyric poet.' That seems to confuse length and genre with profundity. I'm not at all sure, for instance, that Mavis Gallant doesn't say as much about totalitarianism in any single story from *The Pegnitz Junction* as Pasternak says in the whole of *Dr. Zhivago*.

At this time, I can't agree with you when you claim that Ling Feng-Mien's painting 'expresses nothing but the wash of colour and the sumptuousness of *sumi* ink'. (I am, of course, at a disadvantage here, since I haven't seen this particular work, but I generalize from what I know of Chinese art.) You claim that 'Michelangelo's work expresses ideas while Ling Feng-Mien's doesn't'. But doesn't it? May not the whole Chinese tradition of thought and feeling, all its assumptions about man and nature, about art in its relation to *tao*, suffuse this watercolour in the same way that *David* embodies the cultural ideals of the Renaissance? You may get more personal satisfaction from one rather than the other, but by what right can you – or Sam – favour one over the other? I suspect that Ling Feng-Mien, in his artistic but non-philosophical fashion, has 'something to say' – perhaps a good deal to say – about Java sparrows, wisteria boughs, and the redeeming human capacity to take pleasure in such things.

And at this point (doubt as you may), Rudy Wiebe can contribute to the debate. In 'The Cloister of the Lilies', the eighth chapter of *The Blue Mountains of China*, a party of Russian guards with their prisoners stops for the night at a ruined building somewhere in Siberia and discovers faint traces of a picture on 'the mucked wall':

> Level with a man's eye on the leaning wall was a design. The Cossack rubbed away grime between cracks and they saw a long row of them burst in a sudden pure white on what could once have been a gray wall.
> 'What the hell is that?' Palazov said.
> 'A flower, a row of flowers ...' Dimitri held a burning stick closer.
> The Cossack was still rubbing. 'Here, here's a big one', he said.
> They all stared.
> Friesen said finally, 'That's white lilies. The stem bends like that and that's the white lily. The big one half cracked is like for a center, you know, here.'
> 'Small balls in hell', Palazov said.

They have stumbled upon a dilapidated cloister; the lilies are symbols not of hell but of heaven. A foul-mouthed guard soon adds his hand-and-rifle-barrel etching to convert sacred emblem into obscene graffito, but the image of the lilies surviving beneath the secular dirt proves, for one Mennonite prisoner, almost miraculously sustaining.

Art, and the artistry that presents art. (But more of that later.)

2. On 'Something to Say'

I HAVE NO INTENTION of trying to adjudicate between Sam and yourself on the 'novel versus short story' topic. While not, I hope, fence-sitting, I find myself occupying ground somewhere in the middle. Though I tend to agree with Sam that a fine short story can hardly compare (if only in the quality of magnitude) with an equally fine novel, I see no reason why a creator of fine short stories should be deemed any less important than a fine novelist. In my view, short story writers should be judged, along with novelists, as *writers.* But they should also be judged, I have no doubt, on what they have to say as well as how they say it.

'Yes – oh dear yes – the novel tells a story' (E.M. Forster, regretfully). I'll risk an adaptation: 'Yes – oh dear yes – both novel and short story have something to say.' I'm not referring to any slick moral or any detachable message but to a quality I can only describe, inadequately, as 'vision'. I can't accept any aesthetic stance that smacks of 'art for art's sake' (even yours), because it seems to me that one of the greatest threats to art is triviality. As a teacher, of course, I'm familiar with the banality of the opposite extreme. We have all grieved over the final paragraph of innumerable freshman essays: 'In conclusion, this novel is important because it teaches us that ...' But we do know, surely, what such students mean. *King Lear,* for instance, is not a play that warns the elderly about the dangers of giving up their power and possessions before they die, but it *is* about 'unaccommodated man', about human greed and human power, about authority, love, loyalty, what Edgar calls 'ripeness', and countless other things as well.

Agreed, *King Lear* exists only in the magnificent words that Shakespeare arranged in order to express it. No teacher of Shakespeare who qualifies as competent will ever roam too far from the words and the art. But one cannot ignore the 'vision', the ennobling wisdom that the words and the art convey. Set against that, the story of the art critic – could it have been Roger Fry? – who is supposed to have pointed to the figure of Christ in Majesty in the centre of a religious painting and said: 'Now this interesting mass ...' That is what can happen if one errs too far in the opposite direction. The painting in question may or may not have been a masterpiece, but the painter was conveying a religious mystery, not experimenting with planes or proportions. Any critical judgement which ignores the subject and the intention (which may not, of course, have been realized) will be incomplete.

I'm not talking about themes; I'm talking about profundity.

But even if a writer has 'something to say', another question arises: is it worth saying? This brings me into dangerous territory. However, here goes.

In the extract you quote from *The Blue Mountains of China* (and I'll be returning to your judgement of Wiebe's novel in due time), Elizabeth Driediger is discussing two contemporary Canadian novels with a friend. One is Stephen Vizinczey's *In Praise of Older Women*; the other, Leonard Cohen's *Beautiful Losers*. Both seem relevant at this point in my argument. Vizinczey's book is crisply, even elegantly written; you would, I'm sure, give it more marks for style than any novel by Wiebe. But dare I suggest, in this age of sexology and dial-a-porn, that, as Vizinczey portrays more and more middle-aged matrons either seduced or seducing, it all becomes ... well ... *boring*? Yes – oh dear yes – the novel has something to say, and in this case it's banal. While reading it, I found myself recalling a remark Robertson Davies once made to a *Time* interviewer. Sex, he observed, 'is like singing madrigals – it's more fun to do than to attend a concert of'. (Not Davies at his most polished stylistically, but the remark of a wise man.) Or, as his mentor George Bernard Shaw wrote on another occasion: 'He who can, does ...'

In Praise of Older Women may, for all I know, be the centre of an underground cult somewhere, but it has surely found its own undistinguished level in the years since Wiebe wrote. As for *Beautiful Losers*, its author remains a name but the novel has slipped somewhat from its pedestal since those heady days when Desmond Pacey (jumping prematurely onto the band-wagon) hailed it in *Canadian Literature* as 'the most intricate, erudite, and fascinating Canadian novel ever written'. Taking down my reading-copy that I haven't opened for years, I find my earlier pencilled, heretical comment: 'The brilliance of the style *almost* redeems the feebleness of the subject-matter.' And (more pompously): 'This book may well be a refutation of the too-easily-articulated belief that all subjects are equally possible for art.' I also find it described, in an excerpt from a review proudly reproduced by McClelland and Stewart on the back cover of my NCL copy, as 'an invitation to play Russian roulette with a phallic pistol'. I can't think of a better summary (far more to the point than Pacey's). The only trouble is – I don't want to.

This brings me to Marian Engel's *Bear* and your own 'Private Parts'. *Bear* is an interesting case because almost every critic who has discussed the book, whether the ultimate judgement has been pro- or anti-, has commented favourably on its style. Fair enough, but a book about a woman who tries to make love to a bear doesn't invite comment purely on its stylistic dexterity. I have been amazed, while reading the commentators (in an effort to understand why anyone would find the book worth talking about) to discover that it's seriously offered as a moral fable about the boundaries between human and animal worlds. Lou *learns,* apparently, that there are limits beyond which one mustn't go. And fucking bears is one of them. Am I being obtuse in suggesting that anyone who doesn't know this before opening this Governor-General's-Award-winning novel (which Engel admitted was begun as an exercise in pornography) is in deep trouble?

There are, I suppose, some people unable to distinguish between the quality of *Bear* and the quality of 'Private Parts', yet anyone who reads your novella as sexually titillating – or, worse, liberating! – stands self-condemned as a bad reader. I would argue, however, that its effectiveness is not merely a result of your stylistic mastery (though that obviously plays a major part in its overall success). I have no doubt of its literary quality, but in what does the artistry consist? There is something appallingly presumptuous about my lecturing you on the merits of your own work, but let my try. 'Private Parts' is an anthology of adolescent (and, in part, post-adolescent) sexual fantasies, inquiries, and allusions, but there is a touching pathos surrounding the whole narrative, a kind of tender melancholy. In particular, I cherish it as a model of tonal control. Some sections are hilarious ('it is to Billy Graham that I owe my first brush with a girl's private parts'), but a fine sense of paradox enables you to blend these moments into a larger structure of elegiac humour and wistful regret. There is something almost irresistibly poignant about the speaker's insecure but single-minded curiosity. The testimony of Freud is here humanized, delivered from the psychoanalyst's office into a real world of personal bewilderment and existential loneliness. The grotesquely absurd and the painfully urgent, balanced.

I'm sorry to have to say this, John, but one of the supreme qualities of 'Private Parts', along with style and grace and humane delicacy, is that it has 'something to say'. And, unlike *Bear*, something worthwhile.

3. On Binary Computers

AS I UNDERSTAND IT, the argument between you and Sam centres upon the construction of mutually exclusive but equally hierarchical aesthetic structures. According to Sam, your position is riddled with ulterior motives, a classic example of the writer turned critic in order 'to argue the case for his own work, to squeeze it into the canon'. In other words, since you don't write 'epic fiction' (the title, incidentally, of my book on the artistry of Rudy Wiebe), you concoct an aesthetic that acknowledges the supremacy of the short story. If you were a painter, you'd be found cross-legged in deep woodland staring at the delicate leaf-shapes of maidenhair ferns, not perched precariously on scaffolding in the Sistine Chapel converting the ceiling into a microcosm of human and divine history. No, not entirely fair, but it's only a slightly heightened caricature of how others see you. Besides, your own caricature of Sam (and I get caught in some of the cross-fire) is at least as extreme: a befuddled academic seeking out pretentious 'great thoughts', dutifully measuring degrees of high seriousness, exchanging stylistic jewels for a humdrum pot of message.

But you go on from there to make what, for me at least, is a very strange deduction. You assume that Sam probably doesn't share your admiration for Nathanael West, V.S. Naipaul, or Paul Scott. You've already speculated that he would 'genuinely *like*'

David and the Giotto frescoes and the Sistine Chapel, while you registered some reservations. In other words, you profess to see the argument in terms of either / or: Michelangelo versus Ling Feng-Mien; D.H. Lawrence in this corner, Evelyn Waugh in that; long novels matched with short stories; large statements stacked against a concern for semi-colons; the dome of St. Peter's compared to an exquisitely designed door-knob; Rudy Wiebe downgraded in favour of (God save the mark) Elmore Leonard.

Either / or. Binary. Computer distinctions.

My own responses just don't fit into this neat pattern. (I suppose a computer would categorize me as a both / and man.) Let me cite an example from literature. Between attending the short story conference at Guelph and writing this paper, I've been discussing with my second-year undergraduate class in Canadian fiction Hugh MacLennan's *The Watch That Ends the Night* and Sheila Watson's *The Double Hook*. Now where I assume that we can agree is in the observation that MacLennan (all too obviously, I hear you saying) has 'something to say' – in your sense of the term though not necessarily in mine – while Watson hasn't. So far, so good. But if you were to conclude from this that I prefer *The Watch* to *The Hook*, you'd be wrong. I am not required to teach either novel; I choose to assign both because I consider them excellent examples of almost diametrically opposed types of fiction (and, coincidentally, published within months of each other). I think that students should be exposed to these extremes on the spectrum of fictional kinds, that they should be encouraged to consider them and come to some conclusions about them.

Now I realize, of course, that if one is looking for artistic detachment, *The Double Hook* wins hands down. It seems to me a virtual archetype of modernism, comparable with Eliot's poetry, Beckett's *Waiting for Godot*, Henry Moore's sculpture, Rouault's *Miserere* prints, Poulenc's *Dialogues of the Carmelites*, as representative of a well-defined period in twentieth-century western culture. A writer's novel. By contrast, from a rigorously stylistic or aesthetic viewpoint, *The Watch* is deeply flawed. Yet the last few chapters of *The Watch* – didactic, authorially intrusive, blundering in their elementary narrative strategies, verging on the sentimental, positively Victorian in their bourgeois earnestness – are among the most moving and impressive pages of fiction I have ever read. MacLennan is fumbling towards 'something to say', something so momentous that the fumbling no longer matters, is itself part of the experience. If those chapters do not measure up as 'art', then so much the worse for art.

There, I've admitted it. And I want to acknowledge immediately that I've been emboldened to write this (thank God I've got tenure!) because you were courageous enough in 'Dear Sam' to voice your own puzzlements and contradictions. This makes me suspect that, basically, we're not all that far apart. Let me quote you:

> ... I've always believed and taught that the way to connect with that life [i.e., 'what Wilde calls "an independent life"'] is through an appreciation of the artificialities of technique and rhetoric. At the same time, however, I believe that the purpose of art is moral and that the effect of art is moral.
>
> This would seem to be contradictory. Let us not beat about the bush. It *is* contradictory. This problem has troubled me since I was about eighteen.... My solution to the problem, arrived at after years of thought, was simply to stop thinking about it. I now say, at a brisk pace and hoping I won't be challenged, that although one's responses to art are aesthetic ones, these aesthetic responses convert themselves into emotional responses of a different kind, responses which connect us with the real world.

Well, *I* won't challenge you; I agree up to the hilt. On the contrary, I cannot be too grateful to you for your brave if vulnerable honesty. It takes devotion, selflessness, and integrity to risk a confession of that kind. Whatever our other differences may be, here I'm glad to be your disciple.

But the supposed ineptitude of Rudy Wiebe: that's another matter. I'll challenge you there.

4. On Parts and Wholes

IN YOUR ENDEAVOUR to make a case against Rudy Wiebe, you quote three lengthy sections from his work. I shall confine myself, however, to the extract from *The Blue Mountains of China*. After all, the remarks of mine to which you take exception are contained in an introduction to that novel published eight years before the appearance of *My Lovely Enemy*, from which your other examples derive. My arguments could be applied or adapted, I believe, to the later novel as well, but I have also expressed the opinion that *The Blue Mountains* is Wiebe's finest novel to date. If I can't find a chink in your armour here, my case is lost.

Before I turn to the text itself, however, the image of Laocoön rises before me, provoked (as I now realize) by your quotation from Alice Munro. Something clicks, and I remember why an impression of that statue lay close to the surface of my consciousness. A day or two earlier, I had been reading Louis Dudek's recently published *In Defence of Art*. In 'The Revelation of Photography as Art and as Witness', he articulates his own ideas about *kinesis* and *stasis* in terms of moving films and still photographs as ways of 'pretending to represent "reality"':

> The German critic and dramatist Gotthold Ephraim Lessing in his *Laokoon* tried to distinguish between the different arts in this way, and he actually discussed the problem of why a particular moment, in painting or sculpture, is the right moment at which the action is to be arrested and depicted. His model was the sculpture of Laocoön and his sons in the coil of the serpent, and he had many interesting points to make, about the nature of that particular moment, just preceding agony. Today, we would say that the ideal

moment, for the camera, or the imagist poem [or, may I interpolate, the short story?], is at epiphany – a moment of revelation which is numinous in some way, an ecstasy, as any action or moment can be in a work of art. I think of Keats' arrested moment in the Grecian Urn, in which the lover is about to kiss the girl and is stopped just there. 'Forever wilt thou love, and she be fair!'

That passage has obstinately fused in my mind with Alice Munro's extraordinary statement about how she wants her stories to be read, which you – incredibly, so far as I'm concerned – quote as speaking for yourself and for other imaginative writers:

> I will start by explaining how I read stories written by other people. For one thing, I can start reading them anywhere; from beginning to end, from end to beginning, from any point in between in either direction. So obviously I don't take up a story and follow it as if it were a road, taking me somewhere ...

Frankly, I'm flabbergasted! I think of the opening of your own 'Polly Ongle' which you read so effectively at one of the conference readings: 'Paul Denton's morning erection was thrusting the sheet into a comic tent.' As a literary critic, I would want to say that there you have found – by a brilliant stroke, unquestionably – 'the right moment at which the action is to be arrested and depicted'. Or 'Gentle as Flowers Make the Stones', sensitively analysed by James Harrison earlier the same day, which begins: 'Fists, teeth clenched, Jim Haine stood naked and shivering staring at the lighted rectangle.' Did you plan these stories, organize them, arrange them, mould the words and rhythms to achieve the best possible initial impact – just so that Alice Munro can start at the end or in the middle? Are you trying to tell me that you are indifferent to form?

But what, you may ask, does all this have to do with Wiebe, *The Blue Mountains of China,* and his supposed 'tin ear'? Quite a lot.

The extract you quote begins on page 182 of a novel that contains 227 pages in all. It occurs in the last of thirteen chapters, and you've chosen to start one page into the chapter. That's fair enough, I suppose, if it doesn't matter where you start. But suppose it does matter. What if Wiebe's sense of form (dare I suggest it?) is finer here than yours? What if the effect of this passage depends, at least to some extent, on its position within the whole?

This is how Wiebe *begins* his novel – with a voice (and we have to find out where it comes from):

I have lived long. So long, it takes me days to remember even parts of it, and some I can't remember at all until I've been thinking over it a little now and then for weeks, and little Johann or Friedl ask, 'Urgrossmuttchi, what is that, so cold in Canada the ground is stiff?' Then I have to be careful or I'll start making it up, they like to hear so much. What I tell I remember only through God's grace.

A tin ear? Surely not. That is a human voice, a woman's, a fumbling but strangely eloquent broken English. Some years ago in *The Globe and Mail,* Wiebe remarked of this chapter that he had 'tried to capture both the contorted language and self-deprecating humour of prairie Mennonites'. The contortedness, then, is deliberate; it can't just be dismissed as 'ponderous and inept'. It's part of a *design.*

Frieda Friesen's voice is the first of many voices we hear in the course of the novel. One belongs to the father of a family who deserts his son in a desperate attempt to get out of Russia; he fails, and spends years as a prisoner in Siberia (where he encounters the cloister of the lilies). A young, headstrong, rather flighty girl is more fortunate, and we see her growing painfully into womanhood on her voyage across the Atlantic. There are others, men and women, old and young, courageous and timid, well-spoken and inarticulate. A motley collection, but paradoxically united: they are all Mennonites, and they all suffer.

The final chapter opens in (of all unlikely places) Toronto International Airport:

> Elizabeth had perhaps ten minutes to plane time when she noticed the old man in difficulty. She sat too far away to hear them, but the man's clothes, beyond the obvious distress of the two airline agents, left no doubt he was a foreigner; probably – oh, most likely Iron Curtain. She didn't much relish getting up; Toronto International Airport no less and it would be doing well if at any given moment it could officially muster someone who spoke French....

Once again, the subject is language, and the passage you quote is presented as a flashback to a morning conversation. Elizabeth, the central consciousness in this section, is herself a professional linguist; and, as soon as she is addressed by the 'familiar childish name' of Liesel, we recognize her as the independent young girl on shipboard. (For a writer with what you call a '*barbarous*' prose, Wiebe can convey a surprising amount with a single word.) Moreover, with the sentence immediately following the end of your excerpt, we return to the old man at the ticket-counter, who is eventually identified as Jakob Friesen, Frieda's cousin, who has survived Siberia. Soon, Jakob and Elizabeth become part of a brief chance reunion, by the side of an Alberta highway, of representatives of the scattered Mennonite families whose wanderings, within the tragic diaspora of our century, the novel has chronicled. The design, you see, is intricate. To isolate a segment is to risk doing violence to the whole.

But let us now look a little more closely at the passage you quote. The two women stumble accidentally into a discussion involving sex and are both embarrassed. What is said is clearly less significant than what is *not* said, what *can't* be said, and what is left tantalizingly implied. Questions are asked but more often deflected than answered. The result is a nervous, staccato, hiatus-filled, truncated conversation. Awkward, to be sure, though it wouldn't be quite so enigmatic if a line hadn't dropped out of the text early on – a circumstance for which McClelland and Stewart must bear the brunt of the blame. After the fourth paragraph of your excerpt, the following should be inserted (restored from typescript):

> 'Why? I'm sure he's heard of it! It's been out almost two years.'

Oddly enough, I have no desire to improve on your own description of 'the simpering and tee-hee quality of the dialogue'. That phrase catches the effect admirably – an effect that comes, however, from artistry and not from ineptitude.

Elizabeth is a professor (moreover, a professor of linguistics), Rachel a professor's wife, yet they are unable to express their humanity – at least on this most human of subjects – with the sincerity and personal directness of the uneducated Frieda Friesen. In the course of this conversation we learn, and Elizabeth learns, that the potentially rebellious young girl on board ship in the fifth chapter has not won through to a genuine independence; she may have abandoned her religious beliefs and principles, but an innate reticence, a basic Mennonite constraint, endures. The scene prepares, inconspicuously, even deftly, for the eventual recognition of the old man at the ticket-counter as a fellow-Mennonite, and their later participation in the curious gathering around the man carrying a cross. Wiebe is looking before and after. Design.

I have already discussed the books that Elizabeth and Rachel themselves discuss in the excerpt. Within the context of the novel as a whole, this passage performs several functions. The bookish references – belligerently secular in the case of Vizinczey, expressive of a perverse form of sexual mysticism in the case of Cohen – ring a discordant change on the numerous allusions to and quotations from sacred scripture that resonate through the rest of the novel. The attempts of the two aging women to be 'modern', 'liberated', 'with it', are by turns disturb-ing, pathetic, excruciating. And by introducing into the body of his text a consideration of the fashionable novels of the time, Wiebe is distinguishing the emphases of his own work, dissociat-ing himself from the supposedly daring subject-matter of fiction in the late 1960s. A lot is going on beneath the (admittedly quirky) surface.

It may surprise you, John, to learn that in ninety-nine cases out of a hundred I would agree with you in your passionately expressed principles about style and technique. But for me Wiebe represents that hundredth case. Yes, I agree with Ray Smith that 'the dichotomy between style and content is false' (which is why I can't accept any evaluation which tries to ignore the content); I agree with Cyril Connolly that critics who down-play style 'are liable to lump good and bad writers together in support of preconceived theories' (but it seems to me that the preconceived theory in this case is yours, not mine). I can't, how-ever, accept your (to me) narrow definition of what constitutes style. Wiebe paints a large canvas, and any detail, a short passage extracted from a larger whole, will not show him to best advan-tage. Unless Ling Feng-Mien represents a very different tradi-tion of Chinese watercolour from the one I have in mind, he will not employ the broad, tortured brush-strokes of a Van Gogh; the exquisite detail of an Andrew Wyeth would be absurdly out of place in a Cézanne (let alone a Harold Town); you don't look for grace and delicacy in a Rodin.

Yes, I'll admit it, there *are* clumsinesses in this passage that I would wish away. Would that a firm copy-editor had persuaded Wiebe to drop some of the more eccentric punctuation, recon-sider some of his word order, smooth out some of the snags in rhythm. Not *all* the awkwardness in the text is necessary to express the awkwardness of the two women. At the same time, *too* polished a style would, in this context, be distracting and inappropriate.

But let's approach the subject from a different direction. In the third section of *What Is A Canadian Literature?* you list the important cultural influences on young writers in Canada in the early 1960s (these young writers would include both Rudy Wiebe and yourself). One of the influences is William Faulkner. I don't want to take up further space making the point here, but I hope you'll agree that it would be possible to take an extract from one of his fictions (no, I don't mean the notorious opening chapter of *The Sound and the Fury*, but a passage from 'The Bear', perhaps, or my favourite, *Absalom, Absalom!*) and make as superficially convincing a case for Faulkner's '*barbarous*' prose as you have made for Wiebe's. But it wouldn't be fair. And consider this. Of the passages you quote from Wiebe, two represent dialogue while the third is an attempt at stream-of-consciousness. Now I would be the first to acknowledge that dialogue is an area where *you* excel (I hear Sam muttering in the background about Metcalf arguing the case for his own work again), and I would not be prepared to say the same for Wiebe – or for Faulkner. When I am in the right mood, Faulkner seems supreme, yet has anyone, even in the deepest cranny of the deep South, ever spoken the way Faulkner makes his characters speak? But does it, ultimately, matter?

Wiebe has written other short stories besides 'Where Is the Voice Coming From?' that merit attention. And he once remarked of *The Mad Trapper* that it showed, among other things, that he could write correct prose when he wanted to. Nonetheless, in search of what you call 'style', I would certainly turn first to yourself (or Hugh Hood or Alice Munro or Clark Blaise). But permit me to say that, for what Wiebe achieves in *The Blue Mountains of China*, *The Temptations of Big Bear*, and *The Scorched-Wood People*, work of formal magnitude, searing vision, and – yes – 'artistry' on a giant scale, I turn in vain to *Going Down Slow* and *General Ludd*. Once again, I'm a both / and man.

We are all the children of our own times and places. Your literary tastes are quintessentially English – and far be it from me, of all people, to object to *that*. But there are other modes, and Wiebe's Western-Canadian prairie mode is as different from yours as anything can be. I suspect that, unconsciously perhaps, you regard Wiebe as 'barbarous' in the original sense of that word – foreign, alien in speech, babbling. By the same token, it is possible that Wiebe might regard you as an effete, semi-colon-obsessed, provincial Eastern-Canadian fretting and chafing over trivial nuances when elsewhere people are suffering and colours need to be pinned to masts. The two of you are at extreme ends of the spectrum – and each would be wrong about the other. For my part, I believe you both to be excellent writers in your totally opposed traditions. Excellent writers and excellent *artists*. I couldn't possibly confine the term 'artistry' to one side only. A healthy literature – especially a healthy Canadian literature – needs both.

My case rests here.

Epilogue

AND LAOCOÖN?

In the last few days, since my dream, I have been reading about the statue of Laocoön in Kenneth Clark's *The Nude*. I'm prepared to bet that you, John, view with a good deal of unease that smooth impressario of high culture, but what he has to say is of some interest. After being lost for centuries, the statue was unearthed in 1506, and Michelangelo was present within hours of its discovery. Clark calls it 'a decisive event in his career as an artist'. This suggests that my subconscious, in evoking Laocoön, is favouring Sam's position – or, rather, the position you attribute to him. On the other hand, Clark notes how artists, poets, critics, and philosophers have all 'read into it their own needs and poetic aspirations', so perhaps I may be allowed to act as my own interpreter. I think that I know now why (thanks in part to Louis Dudek, Alice Munro, and yourself) I had my dream of Laocoön. I see the statue as embodying, in visual terms, the whole controversy we have been engaged in here. Some of the details, to be sure, are glossed over. Forget Laocoön himself as the disobedient priest; forget the relationship of the three figures and the youthfulness of the sons. See rather three human beings caught, agonizingly, in the coils of two serpents. *Any* human beings, but so far as I was concerned, in the early hours of Friday, 16 December, they were Sam, yourself, and myself. We're all in this together.

And the two serpents, of course, were two extremes of Art.

SAM SOLECKI is a member of the Department of English at St. Michael's College, University of Toronto. He was a regular panelist on CBC Radio's ACTRA award-winning *In Other Words,* is a former editor of the *Canadian Forum,* and is now Book Review Editor of the *University of Toronto Quarterly* and Poetry Editor for McClelland and Stewart. A specialist in Eastern European, Canadian, and British literature, he has edited *Spider Blues: Essays on Michael Ondaatje* and *Talkin' Moscow Blues: Essays by Josef Skvorecky,* and has written *Prague Blues: The Fiction of Josef Skvorecky.*

In the past twenty years, JOHN METCALF has earned a reputation as one of Canada's finest writers of fiction, as a passionate and very instructive critic, and as the country's most important anthologizer and editor of short stories. In addition to several books of his own fiction, including his *Selected Stories* and *Adult Entertainment,* he has published two books of criticism, *Kicking Against the Pricks* and *What Is A Canadian Literature?,* as well as numerous textbooks, such as *Making It New* and *Writers in Aspic.*

W.J. KEITH is a member of the Department of English at University College, University of Toronto. A former editor, for many years, of the *University of Toronto Quarterly,* he has written extensively on both British and Canadian literature. His books on British literature include the study *Richard Jefferies* and three acclaimed volumes on rural British non-fiction, poetry, and novels: *The Rural Tradition, The Poetry of Nature,* and *Regions of the Imagination.* His numerous discussions of Canadian literature include the study *Charles G.D. Roberts,* the critical survey *Canadian Literature in English,* and *A Sense of Style: Studies in the Art of Fiction in English-Speaking Canada.* A new volume, *An Independent Stance: Essays on English-Canadian Criticism and Fiction,* is in preparation. W.J. Keith is a Fellow of the Royal Society of Canada.